Corporate Identity 4

4
Mtv Production Development
Mtv Celebrity Talent
Mtv Productions
Mtv News & Specials
CORPORATE COMMUNICATIONS
MTVN TAPE LIBRARY
4

Corporate Identitiy 4

An International Compilation of Corporate Identity Programs
Eien internationale Auswahl von Identitätskonzepten
Panorama international des concepts d'identité institutionnelle

CEO & Creative Director: B. Martin Pedersen

Publisher: Doug Wolske
Publications Director: Michael Gerbino

Editors: Andrea Birnbaum, Michael Porciello
and Heinke Jenssen

Art Director: Lauren Slutsky
Design & Production: Joseph Liotta
and Nicole Recchia

Published by Graphis Inc.

opposite: elevator exterior design for MTV Networks by Looking

QW
BAY

Contents Inhalt Sommaire

Remarks: We extend our heartfelt thanks to contributors throughout the world who have made it possible to publish a wide and international spectrum of the best work in this field. Entry instructions for all Graphis Books may be requested from: **Graphis Inc.**, 307 Fifth Avenue, Tenth Floor, New York, NY 10016, or visit our Web site at www.graphis.com.

Anmerkungen: Unser Dank gilt den Einsendern aus aller Welt, die es uns ermöglicht haben, ein breites, internationales Spektrum der besten Arbeiten zu veröffentlichen. Teilnahmebedingungen für die Graphis-Bücher sind erhältlich bei: **Graphis Inc.**, 307 Fifth Avenue, Tenth Floor, New York, NY 10016. Die aktuellsten Einsendetermine finden Sie unter: www.graphis.com.

Remerciements: Nous remercions les participants du monde entier qui ont rendu possible la publication de cet ouvrage offrant un panorama complet des meilleurs travaux. Les modalités d'inscription peuvent être obtenues auprès de: **Graphis Inc.**, 307 Fifth Avenue, Tenth Floor, New York, NY 10016. Pour les dates limites les plus actuelles consultez www.graphis.com.

 ISBN: 1-888001-70-4 Printed in Hong Kong.

opposite: signage for the City of Long Beach by Sussman/Prejza & Co. Inc.

flowers
TOMMY LUKE
IN THE PEARL DISTRICT. 228-3140

opposite: poster for Flowers Tommy Luke by Sandstrom Design

LONG
DISTANCE
TELEPHONE

AMERICAN TELEPHONE & TELEGRAPH CO.
BELL
SYSTEM
AND ASSOCIATED COMPANIES

The Latest, **Greatest Brand** by Mike Hicks

Many years ago I read a book whose protagonist, upon returning to his old Brooklyn neighborhood, noticed that Feinberg's Funeral Home had changed its name to Death 'N Things. At the time, I thought it was humorous snipe at modernization. Today, I wouldn't be at all surprised to hear the idea proposed in a marketing meeting. It seems so, well, now. "In conclusion, Mr. Feinberg, our proposal puts a positive spin on your core business, makes the public image more user friendly, involves your customers in an interactive pre-burial experience and broadens the retail model towards broader inventory and greater profit potential." The new branding should, of course, avoid family labeling in order to provide the broadest base for franchising. If Death 'N Things doesn't float the boat, The Funeral Barn™ or Caskets 'N Baskets would certainly fit the bill. Large and corporate? Consider Ameritual®. Add a snappy positioning line such as "Put some FUN in your FUNeral" and, given the swelling ranks of the aging baby boomers, you've got yourself a new billion dollar concept: Hereafter Marketing. All you need now is a really hot branding program.

We live in extraordinary times. The Nike swoosh and rainbow-banded Apple logo that heralded the last latest new era now seem so last decade. There are, however, those among us who believe technology is wreaking a terrible toll on our culture. Its constant, exponential evolution is the culprit—depriving us of our privacy in exchange for convenience, burdening us with unimaginable stress in hopes of increased productivity and, worst of all, creating a disposable culture that views virtually all products and services as merely transient. These doomsayers cite the last decade as the first in history whose buildings were designed with no expectation of permanence, whose products were often obsolete within months (if not weeks) and whose consumers were clamoring to swap fundamental rights for new products embodying the very latest cultural caches. They view the preceding decade as an omen, the chrysalis of a short attention span society fluttering from product to product and service to service, perpetually fascinated with the latest and greatest. Bummer. Break out the Prozac.

The silver lining to this admittedly Orwellian cloud is that the scramble of commercial interests to continuously re-package and re-position themselves has created an unprecedented business bonanza for designers of all sorts. Generation D (children of the Baby Boomers and the only generation to grow up totally immersed in digital technology) is the first to have any lasting impact on American culture not by virtue of their numbers, but because of their affluence and influence. They alone have a truly innate and instinctual understanding of technology and its transient nature. They alone embrace the ever-evolving pathway. Old-timers may know the technology, but they will never "feel" it. The Boomers, who created "youth culture," youth marketing and who are now firmly in control of corporate America, are very, very insecure about this fact. Hence, they're repositioning like Hell in an attempt to remain relevant to the youth market, its many older emulators and, to some extent, themselves. In any event, it should come as no surprise that virtually every major corporation in the country is now trying to put a new spin on their old looks. For the most part, this means selecting a strange name (there are no normal names left for which a dot-com URL can be secured) and creating a new identity system that reflects the techno/surfer/slacker look. Ditch the hard-edged monolithic logo and get soft and friendly. Casual. Cool. Approachable. Adaptable.

While it's a little embarrassing to watch the duding-out of corporate America, there is, nonetheless, some interesting and quite imaginative work being produced in the process. Examples of this are everywhere, but none more perfectly demonstrates the phenomenon than Bell Wireless. In my particular corner of the world, that entity was the telephone company formerly known as Southwestern Bell, whose cellular division mutated into Southwestern Bell Wireless. They had the familiar chunky bell-in-a-circle logo that legendary design guru Saul Bass created decades ago and which had come to represent reliability, stability and stifling corporate bureaucracy. Their white vans with the sky blue and puke green graphics were a fixture of the American landscape. At the beginning of the year, this matron of telecommunications was dethroned and replaced by an extremely fun, personal, hip and technologically endowed company called Cingular Wireless. The change came with a soft edged, X-shaped quirky little logo guy and a new orange and white action color scheme. The changeover was handled very professionally, occurring with such speed and thoroughness that it was almost as if, one morning, I woke up in a different country where Bell Wireless never existed. The illusion lasted until I received my monthly statement which, though thoroughly branded, still had the breathtakingly itemized, incomprehensible detail I had come to rely on from Bell.

So while Ma Bell may never truly change, her latest facelift is so utterly upbeat that even looking at my bill seems somehow better…a sort of, like, totally connected, warm and fuzzy experience. That's what good branding is all about. Right?

Mike Hicks is the head of Hixo, Inc., a design firm in Austin, Texas. Over the last 20 years, his work has been featured in every major design show and publication in the U.S. He has written several books, numerous magazine articles and has lectured at a variety of universities and conferences.

opposite: progression of logo (from top to bottom) 1889, designed by Angus Hibbard to a 1939 update to Bass Yager Associates 1969 redesign page 12: the final stage, Cingular Wireless logo 2001, designed by BBDO

Die neuste, grossartigste Marke, **von Mike Hicks**

Vor vielen Jahren las ich ein Buch, dessen Protagonist bei seiner Rückkehr in sein altes Wohnviertel in Brooklyn feststellte, dass Feinberg's Funeral Home (Feinbergs Bestattungsinstitut) sich jetzt "Death 'N Things" nannte. Damals dachte ich, es sei ein humorvoller Seitenhieb auf die Modernisierungsmanie. Heute würde es mich nicht überraschen zu hören, dass die Idee in einer Marketing-Sitzung geboren wurde. Das hätte ungefähr so geklungen: "Zusammenfassend, Mr. Feinberg, sei gesagt, dass unser Vorschlag ihrem Kerngeschäft eine positive Richtung gibt, für ein verbraucherfreundlicheres Image in der Öffentlichkeit sorgt, Ihren Kunden ein interaktives Vorbestattungserlebnis bietet und das Absatzmodell bezüglich Sortiment und Profitpotential erweitert. Beim neuen Branding sollten natürlich Familiennamen vermieden werden, um eine möglichst breite Basis für Franchising-Geschäfte zu gewährleisten. Wenn "Death 'N Things" nicht funktioniert, wäre "The Funeral Barn™" (Die Bestattungsscheune) oder "Caskets 'N Baskets" (Särge und Körbe) sicher sehr erfolgversprechend. Es soll nach einem Grossunternehmen klingen? Wie wäre es mit Ameritual®. Dazu braucht man noch einen guten Slogan wie zum Beispiel "Put some FUN in your FUNeral" (Sorgen Sie für etwas Spass bei ihrem Begräbnis), und schon hat man angesichts der starken, allmählich in die Jahre kommenden Baby-Boomer-Generation ein neues Milliarden-Dollar-Konzept: Marketing für das Danach. Alles, was man dann braucht, ist ein wirklich heisses Branding-Programm."

Wir leben in einer aussergewöhnlichen Zeit. Das Nike-Häkchen und das Apple-Logo mit den Farbstreifen, die die letzte neue Ära verkündeten, sehen jetzt so sehr nach dem letzten Jahrzehnt aus. Es gibt jedoch einige Leute, die überzeugt sind, dass die Technologie einen furchtbar hohen Tribut von unserer Kultur verlangt. Schuld daran ist die konstante, sich exponential entwickelnde Evolution; für die Annehmlichkeiten, die sie bietet, bezahlen wir mit unserer Privatsphäre; in der Hoffnung auf höhere Produktivität wird uns ein unvorstellbarer Stress aufgebürdet, und, was am schlimmsten ist, es wird eine Wegwerfkultur geschaffen, in der praktisch alle Produkte und Dienstleistungen kurzlebig sind. Für diese Schwarzseher ist das letzte Jahrzehnt das erste in der Geschichte, in dem Gebäude ohne die Erwartung von Dauer gebaut wurden, in dem Produkte oft schon innerhalb von Monaten (wenn nicht Wochen) veraltet waren und in dem die Verbraucher bereit waren, Grundrechte aufzugeben für die allerneusten, prestigeversprechenden Produkte. Für diese Pessimisten ist die letzte Dekade ein Omen, Schmetterlingspuppe einer flatterhaften Gesellschaft, die von Produkt zu Produkt, von Dienstleistung zu Dienstleistung fliegt, die unablässig dem Reiz des Neuen, dem scheinbar Grossartigsten erliegt. Was folgt, ist eine harte Landung!

Das Gute an dieser zugegebenermassen orwellschen Wolke ist, dass der wirtschaftlich bedingte Drang zu ständig neuen Verpackungen und neuen Positionierungen für Designer aller Art zu einer Goldgrube ohne gleichen geworden ist. Die Generation D (Kinder der Baby Boomer und die einzige Generation, die ganz mit der digitalen Technologie aufwuchs) ist die erste Generation, die einen bleibenden Einfluss auf die amerikanische Kultur hat. Und das nicht so sehr, weil es sich um eine geburtenstarke Generation handelt, sondern dank ihres Wohlstands und ihrer Fähigkeiten. Nur diese Generation besitzt einen angeborenen Instinkt für die Technologie, sie begreift und akzeptiert ihre Kurzlebigkeit. Nur sie kommt mühelos mit der ständigen Weiterentwicklung zurecht. Die Alten kennen die Technologie vielleicht, aber "fühlen" werden sie sie nie. Die Boomer, die die "Jugendkultur", das Jugend-Marketing erfanden und jetzt in Führungspositionen in der amerikanischen Wirtschaft sitzen, verunsichert diese Tatsache enorm. Also repositionieren sie wie verrückt, in der Hoffnung, auf diese Weise aktuell zu bleiben, für die Jugend wie für die vielen Älteren, die noch dazu gehören wollen, und, in gewissem Masse, für sich selbst. Deshalb überrascht es eigentlich nicht, dass so ziemlich jede grosse Firma in den USA jetzt versucht, ihr Aussehen bzw. das ihrer Produkte aufzumöbeln. In den meisten Fällen heisst das, dass sie sich einen seltsamen Namen ausdenken (es gibt keine normalen Namen mehr, für die man sich ein a.com URL (eine Web-Adresse) sichern kann) und ein neues C.I.-Designprogramm schaffen, das den Techno/Surfer/Slacker-Look reflektiert. Schmeisst das riesige, kantige Logo weg, und werdet weich und freundlich, locker, cool, zugänglich, flexibel.

Diese Bemühungen der amerikanischen Wirtschaftswelt sind zwar etwas peinlich, aber es sind dabei auch einige interessante und phantasievolle Arbeiten entstanden. Beispiele dafür gibt es viele, aber keines demonstriert das Phänomen so perfekt wie Bell Wireless. In meiner Ecke der Welt war dieses Unternehmen ursprünglich als Southwestern Bell bekannt, deren Abteilung für kabellose Telephone zu Southwestern Bell Wireless wurde. Sie hatten ein kreisförmiges Logo, in dessen Mitte sich die vertraute klobige Glocke befand. Der legendäre Saul Bass hatte es vor Jahrzehnten entworfen, und es stand für Zuverlässigkeit, Stabilität – und unflexible Bürokratie. Die weissen Lieferwagen der Firma mit der himmelblauen und schmutzig-grünen Graphik waren Teil der amerikanischen Landschaft geworden.

Anfang des Jahres wurde diese alte Dame der Telekommunikation von ihrem Sockel gehoben und durch eine Firma ersetzt, die locker, persönlich, hip wirkte und technologisch bestens gerüstet war. Ihr Name: Cingular Wireless. Die Veränderung kam mit einem Logo mit weichen Konturen und einer x-förmigen, verrückten kleinen Figur sowie einem neuen, frischen Farbsystem von Orange und Weiss. Der Wechsel wurde sehr professionell gehandhabt, er wurde so schnell und gründlich vollzogen, dass es fast so war, als erwache man eines Morgens in einem anderen Land, wo es Bell Wireless nie gegeben hatte. Die Illusion dauerte an, bis ich meine monatliche Abrechnung bekam, die zwar äusserlich dem neuen Image entsprach, aber noch immer die völlig unverständlichen Details enthielt, die ich von Bell gewohnt war. Wenn also Mamma Bell vielleicht doch im Grunde die Alte geblieben ist, so ist ihr jüngstes Facelifting immerhin so optimistisch, dass selbst der Anblick meiner Rechnung erfreulicher ist. Irgendwie vermittelt sie ein ganz familiäres, warmes, leichtes, unbeschwertes Gefühl. Und nur darum geht es doch bei gutem Branding - oder nicht?

Mike Hicks leitet Hixo Inc., eine Designfirma in Austin, Texas. Während der letzten zwanzig Jahre wurden seine Arbeiten in wichtigen Design-Ausstellungen und Publikationen in den USA gezeigt. Er ist Autor mehrerer Bücher und Zeitschriftenartikel, und er hat an verschiedenen Universitäten und Kongressen Vorträge gehalten.

La dernière grande marque, par Mike Hicks

Il y a plusieurs années, j'ai lu un livre dont le protagoniste avait constaté, en retournant dans son ancien quartier de Brooklyn, que l'entreprise de pompes funèbres Feinberg's Funeral Home s'appelait désormais Death 'N Things. A l'époque, j'ai pensé que c'était une boutade en réaction à la modernisation. Aujourd'hui, je ne serais pas du tout étonné d'apprendre que cette idée a été lancée lors d'une séance marketing. Et le discours tenu à cette occasion ressemblerait, dans les grandes lignes, à ce qui suit: «En guise de conclusion, je dirais, Monsieur Feinberg, que notre proposition, outre le fait qu'elle donnera un aspect positif à votre activité principale et contribuera à véhiculer une image plus conviviale auprès du public, offrira également la possibilité à vos clients de vivre une expérience préfunèbre interactive et élargira le modèle de distribution en termes d'assortiment et de bénéfice commercial. Il apparaît comme évident que la nouvelle marque ne devrait contenir aucun nom de famille afin de garantir une base aussi large que possible en matière de franchisage. Si Death 'N Things ne devait pas faire l'affaire, The Funeral BarnTM (La grange funéraire) ou Caskets 'N Baskets (Cercueils et paniers) devraient rencontrer le succès escompté. Le nom choisi devrait faire penser à une grande entreprise? Que pensez-vous d'Ameritual®? Il suffirait d'y ajouter un bon slogan comme "Put some FUN in your Funeral" (Mettez un peu de FUN dans vos funérailles), et déjà vous aurez, si l'on considère le nombre de baby boomers en passe d'atteindre un âge respectable, un nouveau concept qui vaut des milliards de dollars: le marketing de l'au-delà. Tout ce qu'il vous faut maintenant, c'est un programme de branding percutant.»

Nous vivons à une époque démentielle. Le petit crochet de Nike et le logo d'Apple avec ses bandes de couleur, tous deux annonciateurs d'une ère nouvelle il n'y a pas si longtemps encore, font aujourd'hui tellement «dernière décennie». Certains voient cette évolution d'un mauvais œil, arguant que la culture est sacrifiée sur l'autel de la technologie aux progrès fulgurants. Si cette dernière nous procure un confort certain, nous le payons au prix de notre sphère privée. Qui plus est, elle nous fait subir un stress inouï dans l'espoir d'atteindre une plus grande productivité et, pire encore, elle est à l'origine d'une culture jetable dans laquelle pratiquement tous les produits et services sont condamnés à disparaître bientôt. Les plus pessimistes considèrent la dernière décennie comme la première dans l'histoire où on a construit des bâtiments qui n'ont pas été faits pour durer, où les produits sont devenus démodés en l'espace de quelques mois, si ce n'est de quelques semaines, et où les consommateurs se montraient entièrement disposés à abandonner des droits fondamentaux au profit de produits inédits du dernier chic. Ces oiseaux de mauvais augure voient dans la dernière décennie un présage, la chrysalide d'une société volage qui papillonne d'un produit à l'autre, d'un service à l'autre, et qui succombe immanquablement à l'attrait de la dernière grande nouveauté. L'atterrissage, hélas, est douloureux.

Mais ce qui fait le malheur des uns fait le bonheur des autres: les diktats imposés par les impératifs économiques et commerciaux, à savoir la création débridée de nouveaux emballages et le repositionnement régulier des produits, constituent une manne céleste pour les designers, toutes disciplines confondues. La génération D - les enfants des baby boomers qui sont nés à l'heure de la technologie numérique et ont grandi avec elle - est la première à avoir un impact sur la culture américaine qui s'inscrit dans la durée, non pas en raison de son nombre, mais de son bien-être et de son influence. Seule cette génération possède un instinct inné pour la technologie, en comprend et en accepte la nature éphémère. Et seule cette génération parvient à avancer sans problème sur le chemin de l'évolution constante. Les plus âgés ont beau connaître la technologie, ils ne la "sentiront" jamais. Cet état de fait préoccupe au plus haut point les boomers, les inventeurs de la culture et du marketing pour les jeunes, qui occupent actuellement des fonctions dirigeantes au sein des entreprises américaines. Aussi repositionnent-ils à tous crins dans l'espoir de rester dans le coup, de s'attirer autant les faveurs des jeunes que celles des plus âgés qui souhaitent encore surfer sur la vague. Il n'est dès lors pas étonnant que presque chaque grande société américaine essaie de lifter son image et ses produits. Dans la plupart des cas, cela revient à choisir une raison sociale étrange - il n'existe plus de noms normaux pour lesquels on puisse s'assurer une a.com URL (une adresse Internet) - et à concevoir un nouveau programme de design qui reflète le look techno-surfeur débraillé. Le mot d'ordre est clair: débarrassez-vous de votre logo monolithique dur et sec, et devenez doux, gentil, désinvolte, cool, accessible et souple.

S'il est quelque peu embarrassant d'observer les efforts déployés pour donner une nouvelle image au monde économique américain, il n'en demeure pas moins que des travaux aussi intéressants qu'imaginatifs ont vu le jour au cours de ce processus. Les exemples ne manquent pas, mais aucun ne traduit aussi bien ce phénomène que Bell Wireless. Sur le petit coin de terre que j'habite, cette société était connue initialement sous le nom de Southwestern Bell et sa division pour les téléphones sans fil, sous celui de Southwestern Bell Wireless. Son logo représentait un cercle au milieu duquel apparaissait la cloche massive bien connue de tous. Son auteur, le légendaire Saul Bass, l'avait créé des décennies auparavant. Ce symbole incarnait la fiabilité, la stabilité et la bureaucratie dans toute sa rigueur. Les camionnettes de livraison de la société au graphisme bleu ciel et verdâtre faisaient entre-temps partie intégrante du paysage américain.

Au début de l'année, la vieille dame des télécommunications a toutefois été éjectée de son trône pour céder la place à une société hip, décontractée, personnelle et à la pointe de la technologie. Son nom: Cingular Wireless. Ce changement a bien entendu entraîné la création d'un nouveau logo aux contours doux présentant un petit gars bizarroïde en forme de X dont le nouveau code-couleurs composé de blanc et d'orange se distingue par sa fraîcheur. Cette opération a été menée tambour battant avec un professionnalisme tel que j'ai presque eu l'impression de me réveiller un beau matin dans un autre pays où Bell Wireless n'aurait jamais existé. L'illusion a duré jusqu'à ce que je reçoive mon décompte mensuel qui reflétait certes parfaitement la nouvelle image, mais contenait toujours les détails incompréhensibles auxquels Bell m'avait habitué. Peut-être que dans le fond, Mamma Bell est restée la même, mais le coup de bistouri a si bien réussi que même ma facture me paraît désormais plus sympathique. Elle a quelque chose de familier, de chaleureux, me donne une impression de légèreté, d'insouciance. Et n'est-ce pas là la finalité du branding?

Mike Hicks dirige la société de design Hixo Inc. basée à Austin, au Texas. Au cours des vingt dernières années, le public a pu voir ses travaux dans d'importantes expositions de design et publications américaines. Auteur de plusieurs ouvrages et d'articles de magazine, il donne des conférences dans diverses universités et lors de congrès.

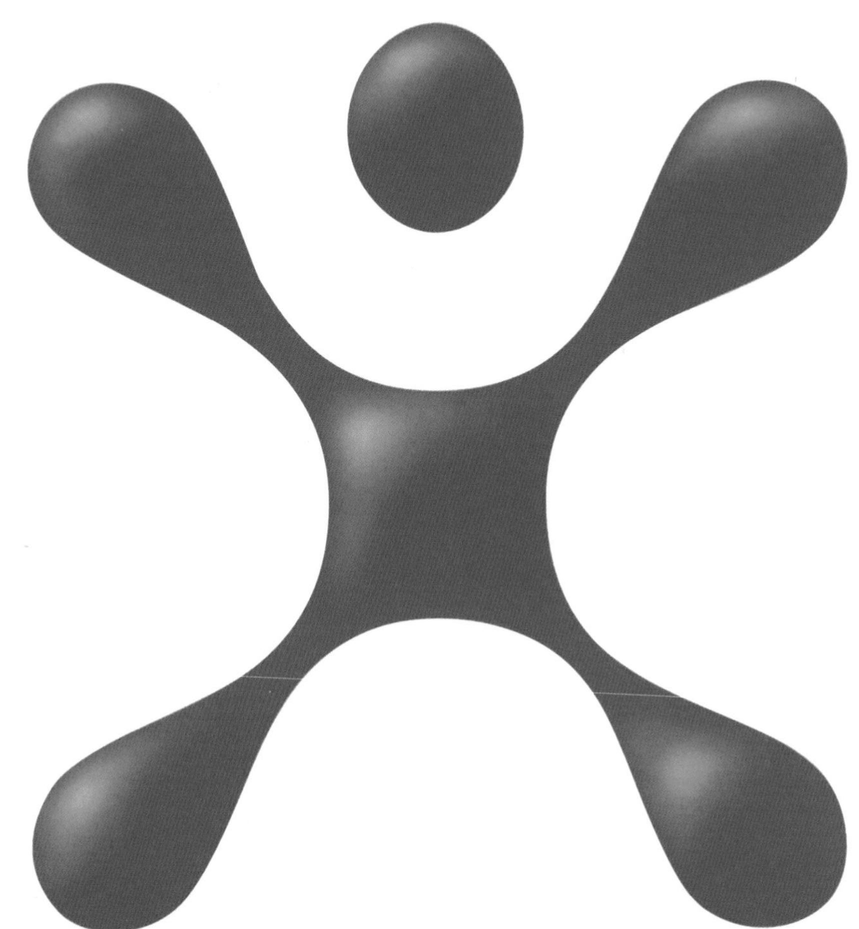

Corporate Identity 4

(this spread) Design Firm **DGWB** Creative Director **Jon Gothold** Design Director **Jonathan Brown** Designers **Jason Simon, Andre Gomez** and **Conan Wang** Architect **Nester & Gaffney** Client **DGWB**

DGWB

MIKE WEISMAN
DGWB
ART SCIENCE ALCHEMY

ALCHEMY

DGWB

(this and following two spreads) Agency **BBI Studio Inc.** Art Director **Zempaku Suzuki** Designers **Zempaku Suzuki** and **Hiroshi Tano** Photographer **Hiroshi Yoda** Copywriter **Nob Ogasawara** Client **Toyo Asano Co., Ltd.**

THE
MISSION
CONSTRUCTING
FOOTHOLDS

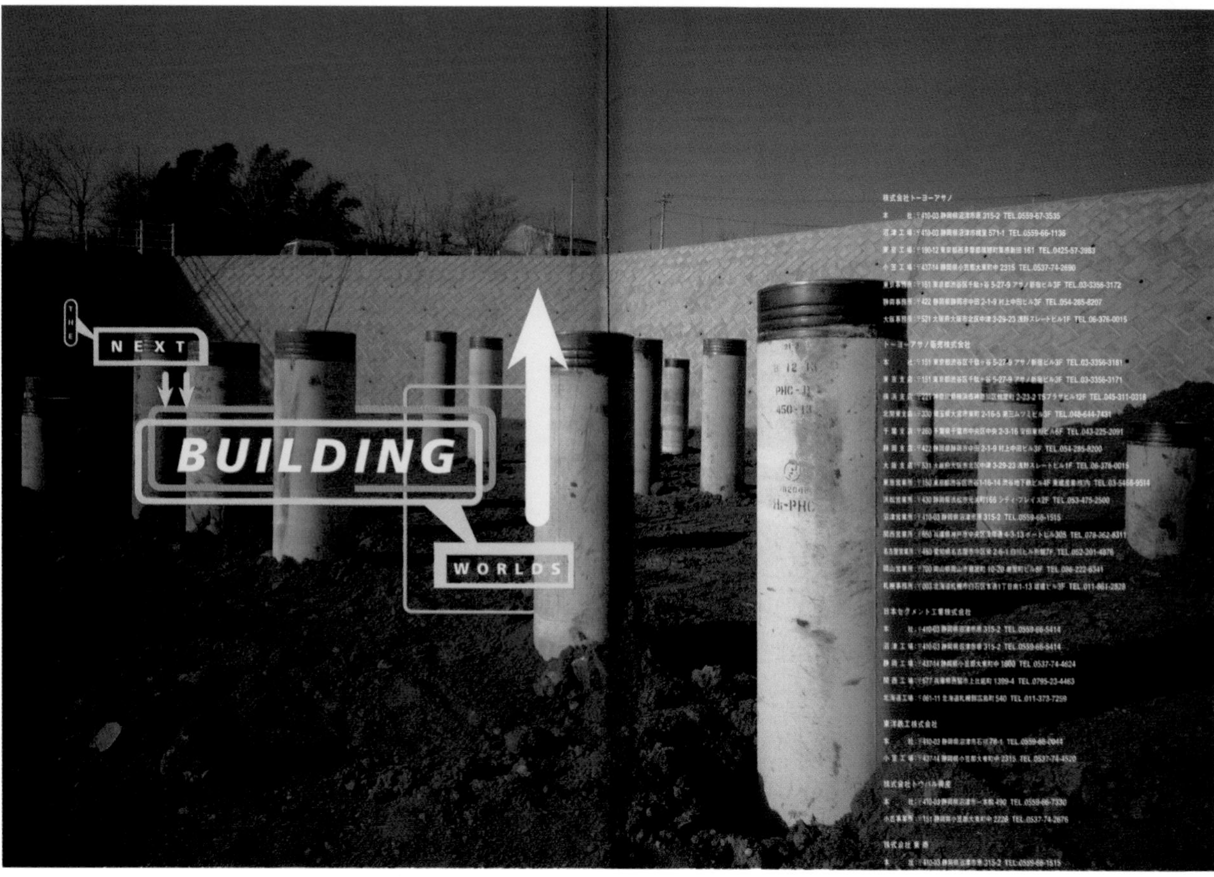
THE
NEXT
BUILDING
WORLDS

TAFCO

A B C D E

F G H I J

K L M N O

P Q R S T

U V W X Y

Z & ! ? “ ” ( )

1 2 3 4 5

6 7 8 9 0

パイル部門

TOYO ASANO
PILES DIVISION

トーヨーアサノの基本は、
安全第一と高品質です。
新しいブランドネーム「TAFCO」には
工場で生産する既成コンクリートパイルと、
施工現場で創り出す現場造成杭があります。
どのような施工条件にも対応できるように、
製品と工法の研究開発には常に余念がありません。
TAFCO-PHCパイル、TAFCO-MCパイル、
TAFCO-STパイル、TAFCO-PRCパイル、
TAFCO-GEMパイル、TAFCO-SCパイルなど、
多種多様な製品群がラインアップ。
同じように、ポールその他
プレキャストコンクリート製品なども含めて、
これまでのゆるぎない実績が
さまざまな工法によって活かされ、
社会資本の基礎づくりにを貢献しているのです。

工事部門

TOYO ASANO
WORKS DIVISION

「TAFCO」の有効活用を追求して、
安全でコストパフォーマンスの高い工法を
研究開発しています。
私たちトーヨーアサノは
基礎杭工事(既成杭、造成杭)をはじめ、
仮設山留工事、アースアンカー工事、
構台仮橋工事、遮壁工事、
薬注工事などの工事技術を最大限に
「基礎」に活かすことを使命としています。
低振動・低騒音のケムン工法や
中掘拡大根固め工法、
多目的掘削工法のCD工法などによって
高い安全性を確保しながら、
工事のスムーズな工程を管理しているのです。

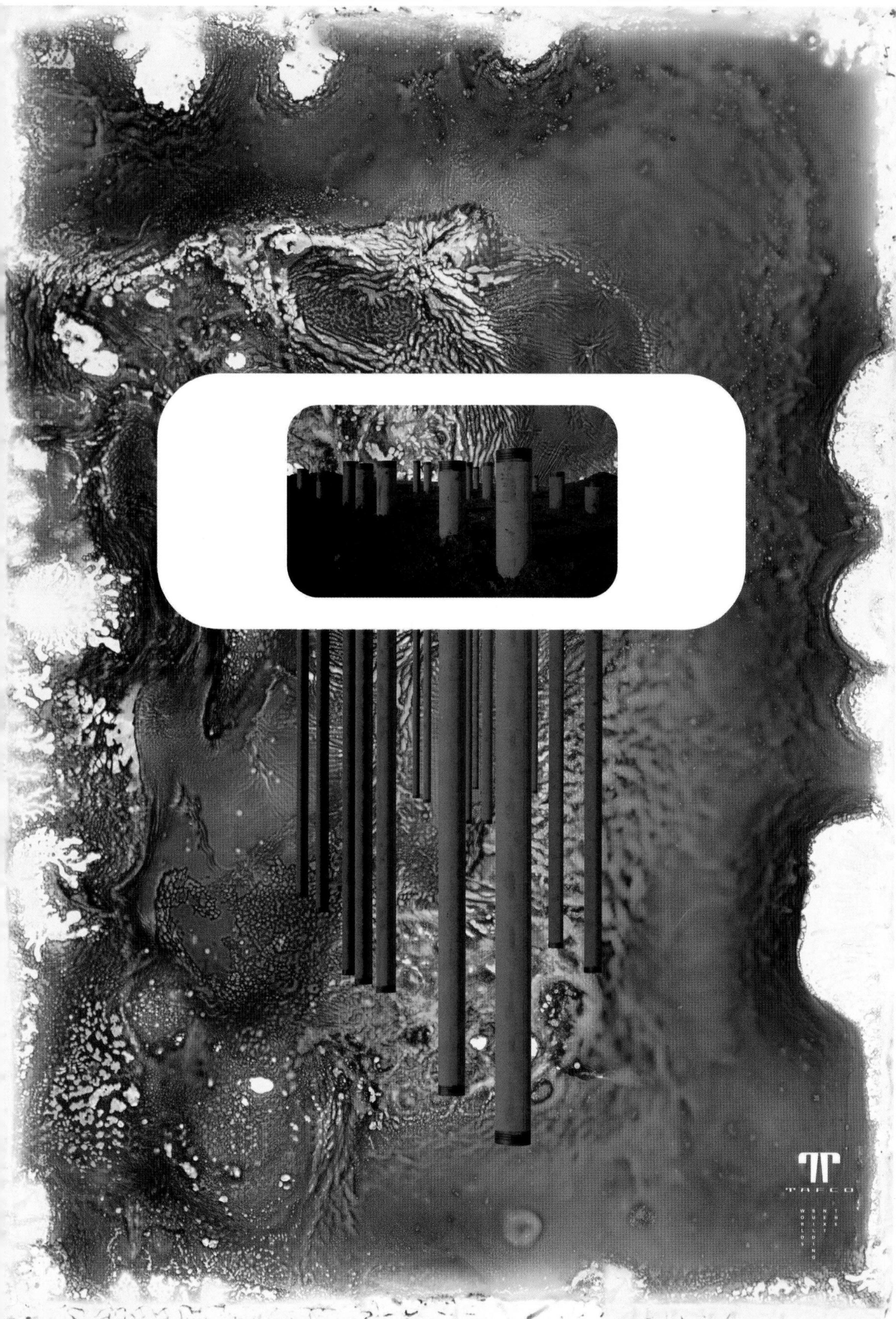
TAFCO
WORLDS
BUILDING
NEXT
THE

(this spread) Design Firm **Duffy Design and Interactive** Creative Director **Joe Duffy** Art Director, Designer and Illustrator **Tom Riddle** Copywriter **John Jarvis** Client **International Transportation Corp.**

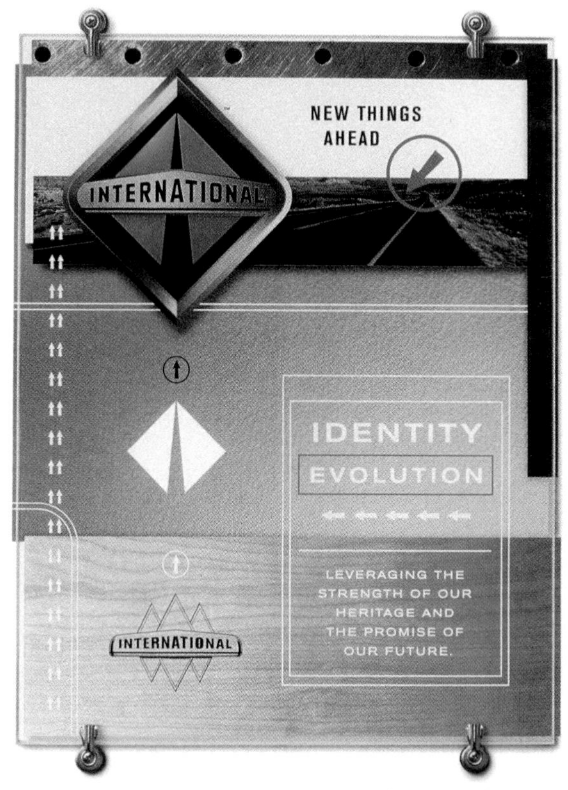
NEW THINGS
AHEAD
INTERNATIONAL
IDENTITY
EVOLUTION
LEVERAGING THE
STRENGTH OF OUR
HERITAGE AND
THE PROMISE OF
OUR FUTURE.
INTERNATIONAL

BENEFITS
consistent identity > commitment to customers > strengthened heritage
NEW
THINGS
AHEAD
INTERNATIONAL
UNDERSTANDING
WHAT CUSTOMERS
EXPECT AND KNOWING
WHAT WE DELIVER.
BRAND
PROMISE
INTERNATIONAL LISTENS, UNDERSTANDS
AND DELIVERS THE BEST WAYS TO MOVE
OUR CUSTOMERS AHEAD. ON THE ROAD
AND IN THEIR BUSINESS.

BRAND
BUILDING
KIT
INTERNATIONAL

INTERNATIONAL
Aa
CD
ENCLOSED

(this spread) Design Firm **Turner Duckworth** Creative Directors **David Turner** and **Bruce Duckworth** Designers **David Turner** and **Allen Ravlet** Client **McKenzie River Corp.**

STEEL.BREWING.COMPANY

HIGH GRAVITY

BACK

HOW TO PLAY:

USE YOUR CURSOR KEYS TO MOVE FROM LEFT TO RIGHT. THE OBJECT IS TO COLLECT 211 POINTS BEFORE YOU GET COMPLETELY SMASHED. YOU HAVE 3 LIVES BUT ONLY 28 SECONDS TO WIN.

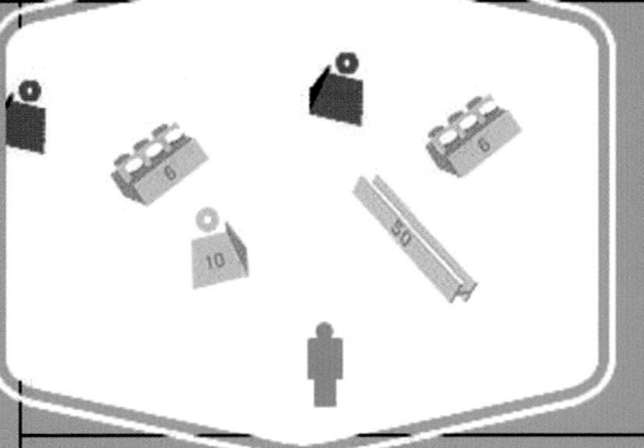

EXTRA MALTED BARLEY & SELECT HOPS FOR EXTRA GRAVITY

LIVES

23 TIME

18 SCORE

SLOW BREWED FOR A MINIMUM OF:

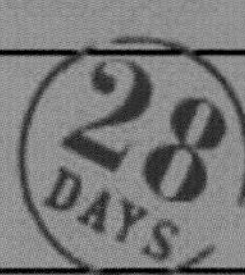

SCORE 211 WITHOUT GETTING WRECKED

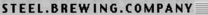

ead) Design Firm **Turner Duckworth** Creative Directors **David Turner** and **Bruce Duckworth** Designer **Anthony Biles** Client **McKenzie River Corp.**

zero°
TM

zero°
FROZEN COLA DRINK
8FL.OZ. (237ml)
zero°
FROZEN CHERRY DRINK
8FL.OZ. (237ml)

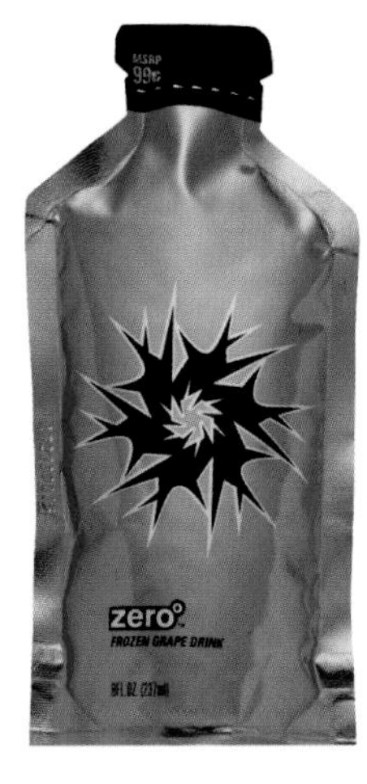
zero°
FROZEN GRAPE DRINK
8FL.OZ. (237ml)

zero°
FROZEN BERRY DRINK
8FL.OZ. (237ml)

(this spread) Design Firm **Lewis Moberly** Art Director **Mary Lewis** Designers **Nin Glaister, Mary Lewis** and **Ann Marshall** Client **Wineworld London Plc**

“BLESS YOU”

VINOPOLIS

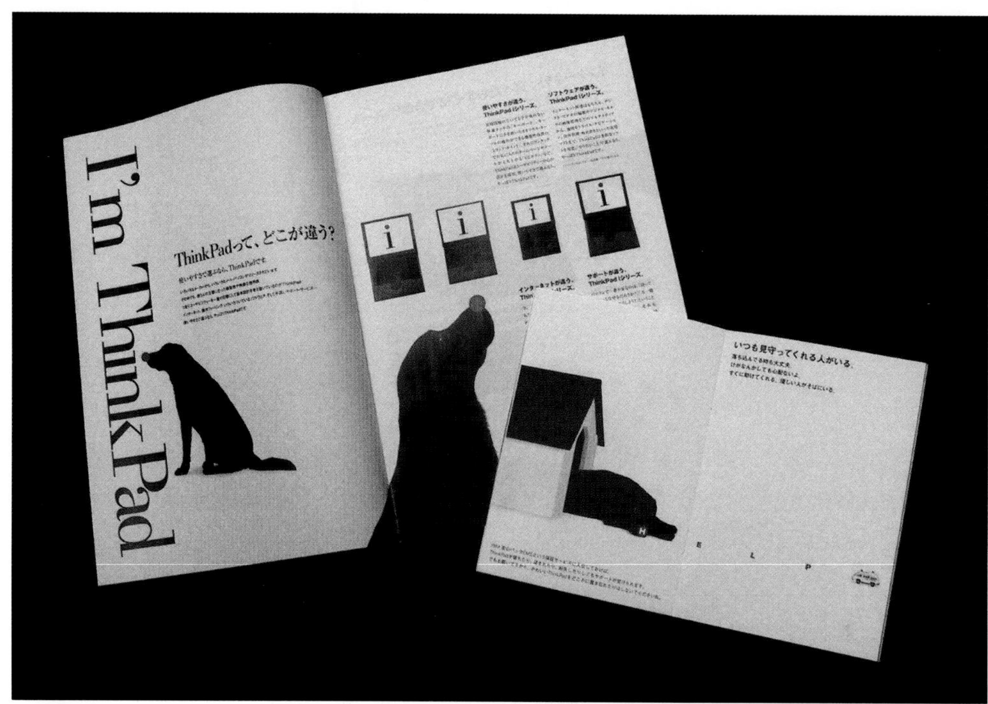

(this spread) Design Firm **IBM Japan Ltd.** Art Directors **IBM Japan, Ltd. Design Center** and **Ken Miki** Designer **IBM Japan, Ltd. Design Center** Photographer **Kazumasa Yamamoto** Copywriter **Yu Hayasaka** Client **IBM Japan, Ltd.**

IBM®

ThinkPad® i Series

Adobe

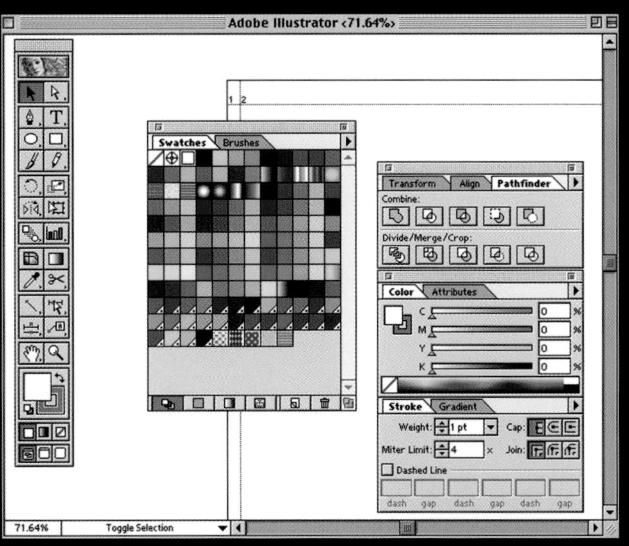

ad Design Firm **Mauk Design** Art Director **Mitchell Mauk** Designer **Ingrid Ballman, Christiane Forsting** and **Gary Helfand** Photographer **Colin McRae** Client **Adobe Systems** (this spread) Design Firm **Turner Duckworth** Creative Directors **David Turner** and **Bruce Duckworth** Designers **Mark Waters, David Turner, Anthony Biles, Sara Geroulis, Mary Koyder** and **Allen Ravlet** Photographers **Lloyd Hyrciw** and **Stan Musilek** Illustrator **Brian Cronin** Client **3Com**

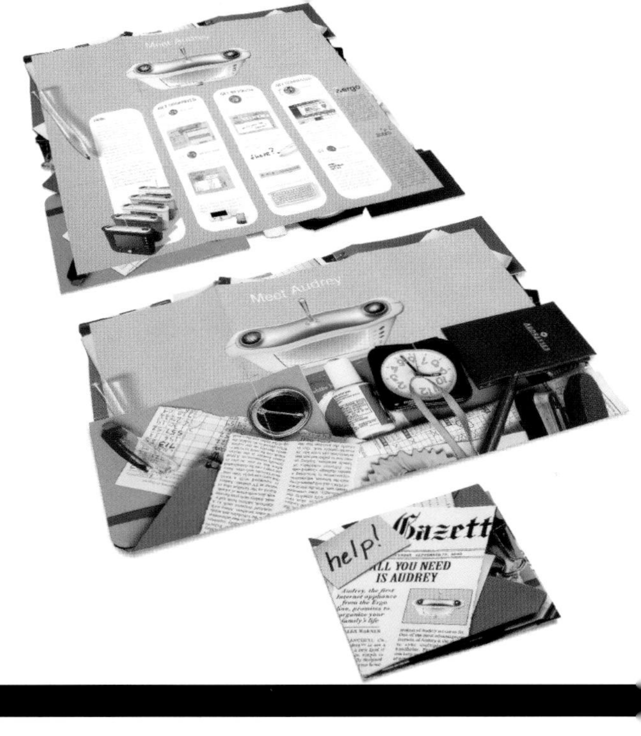
Meet Audrey
help!
ALL YOU NEED
IS AUDREY

ergo
3com
Audrey is
an excellent
communicator
This is Audrey
3com

ergo
AUDREY
This is all you need

(this spread) Design Firm **Lorenc & Yoo Design** Creative and Art Director **Jan Lorenc** Designers **David Park, Steve McCall** and **Susie Caldwell** Photographer **Rion Rizzo (Creative Sources)** Illustrator **Susie Caldwell** Client **Continuum**

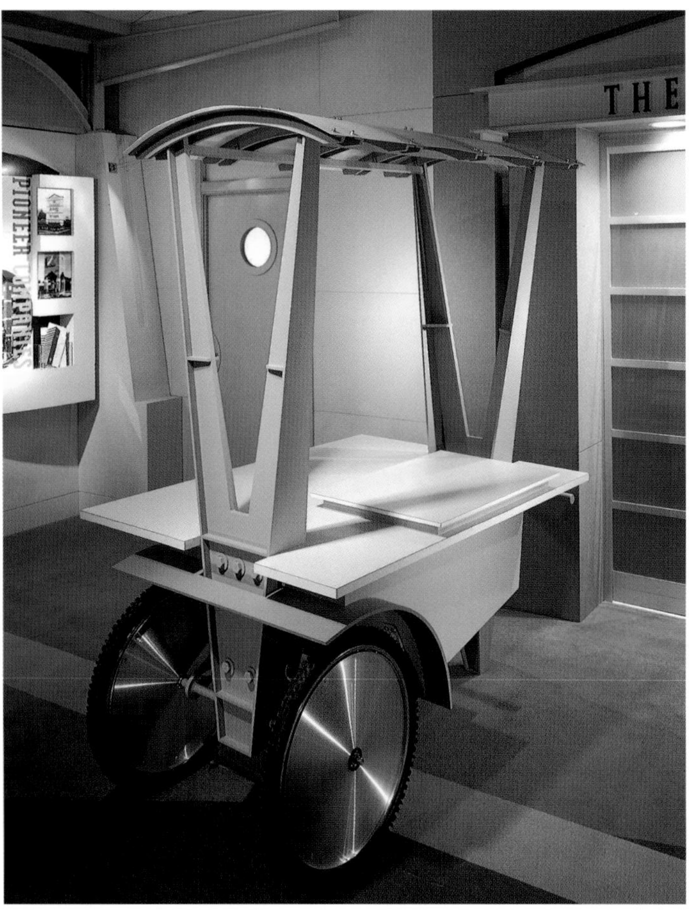

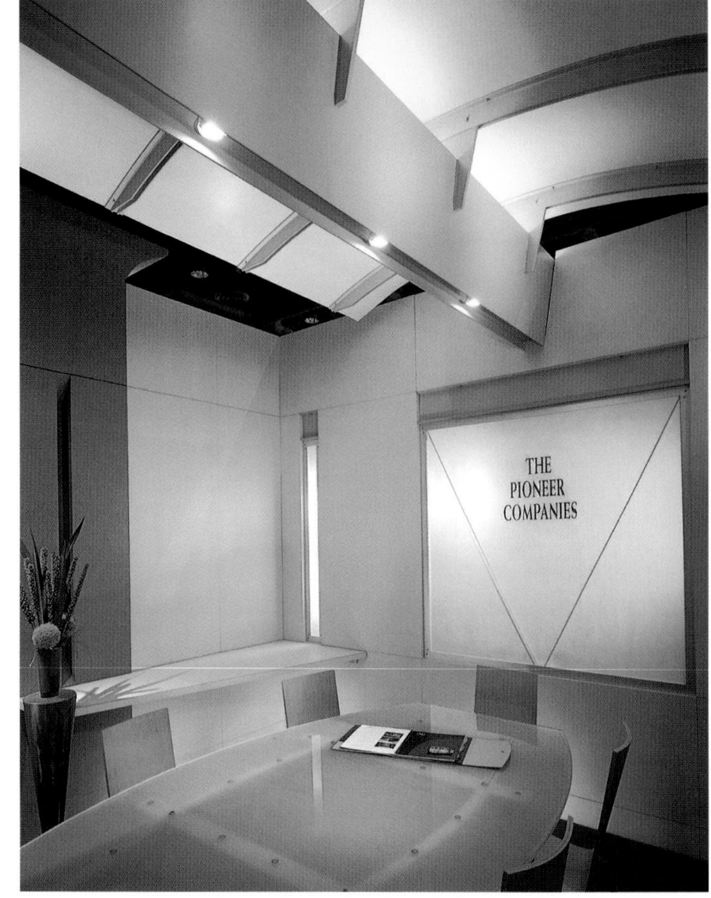

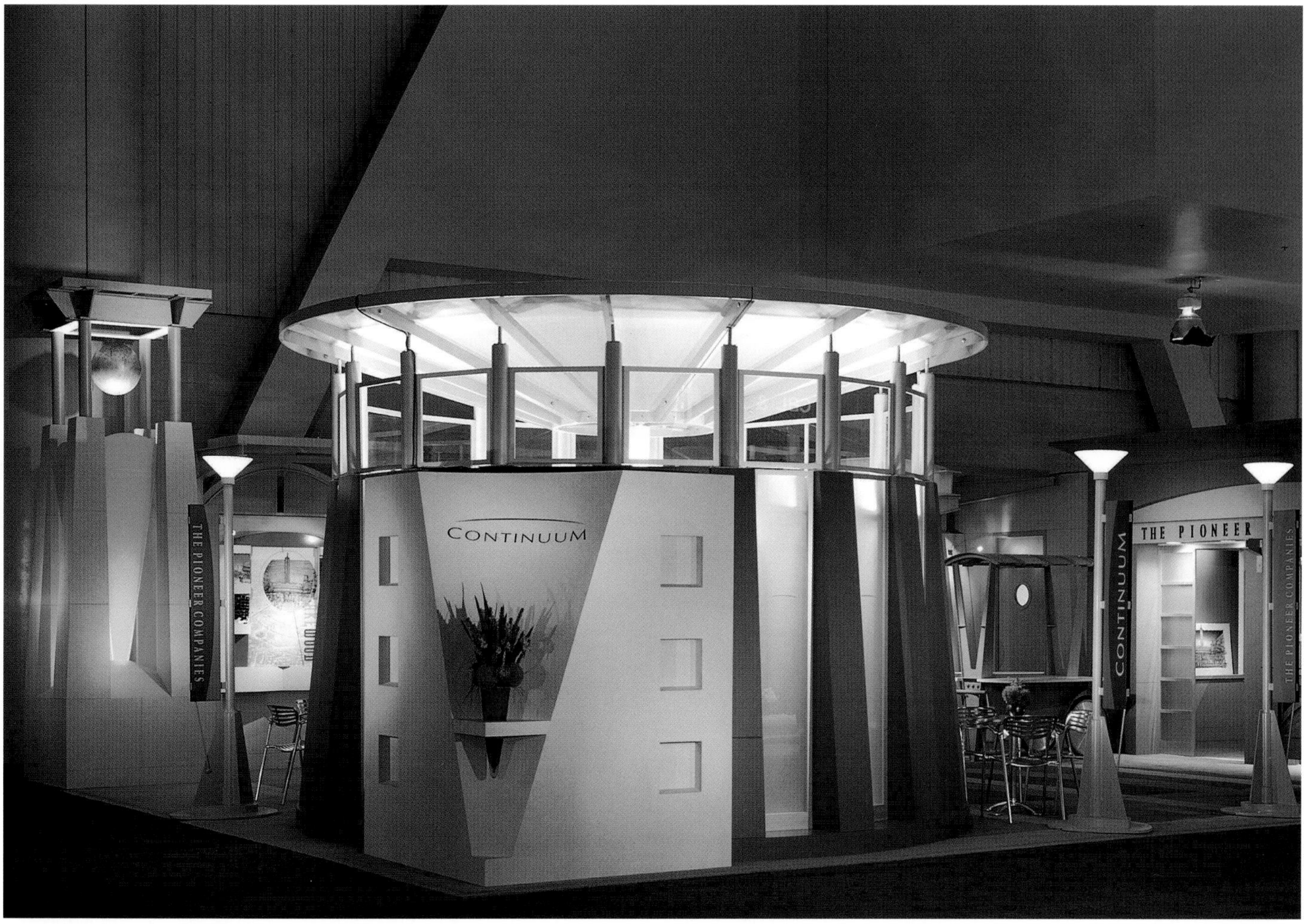
CONTINUUM
THE PIONEER COMPANIES
CONTINUUM
THE PIONEER
THE PIONEER COMPANIES

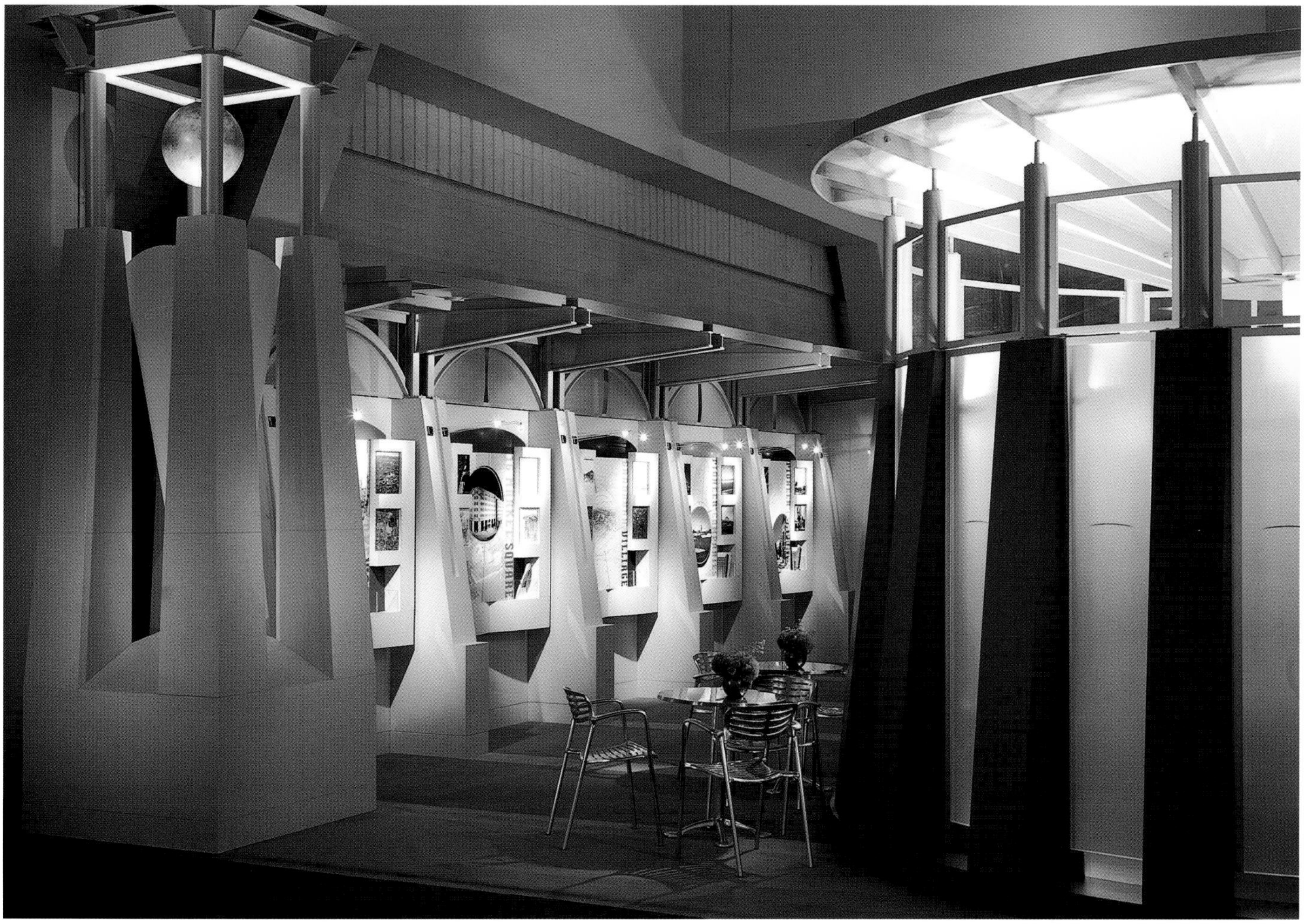

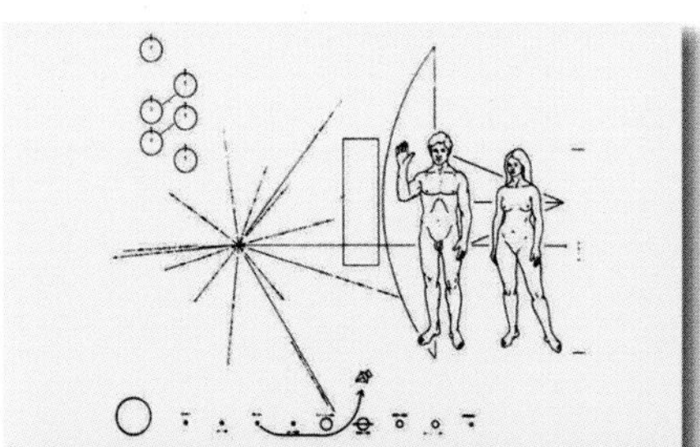

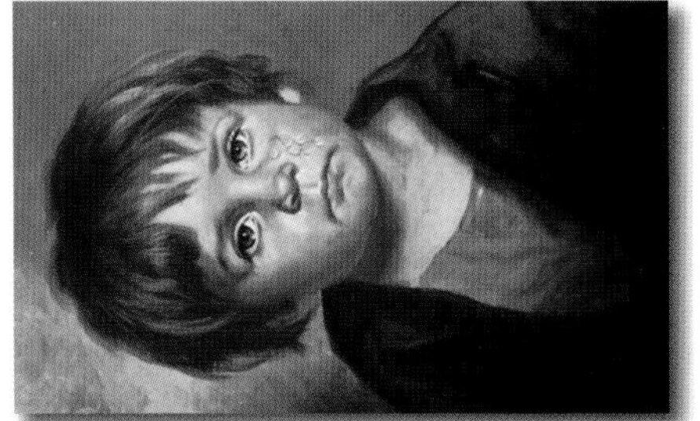
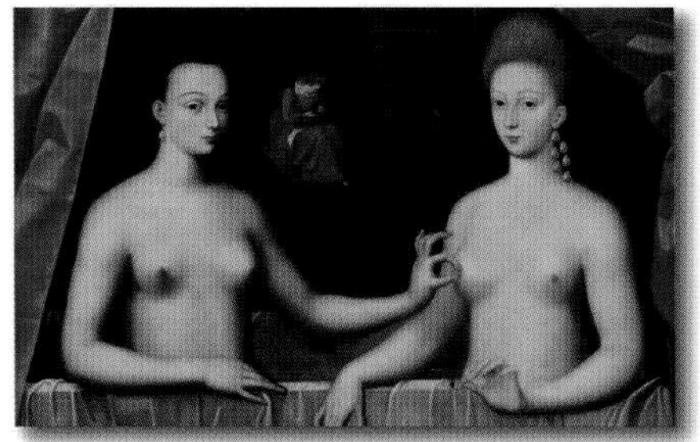

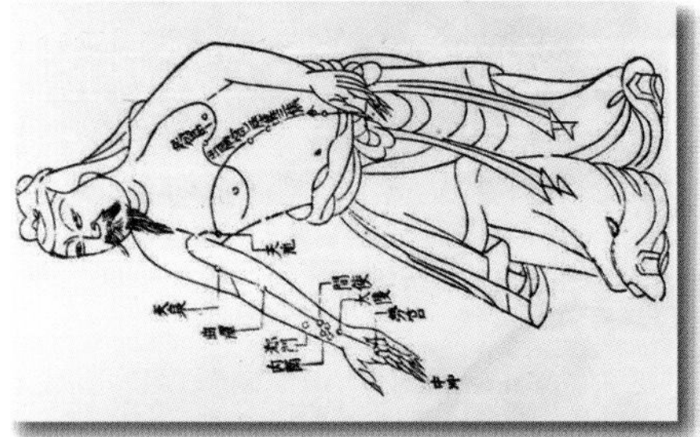

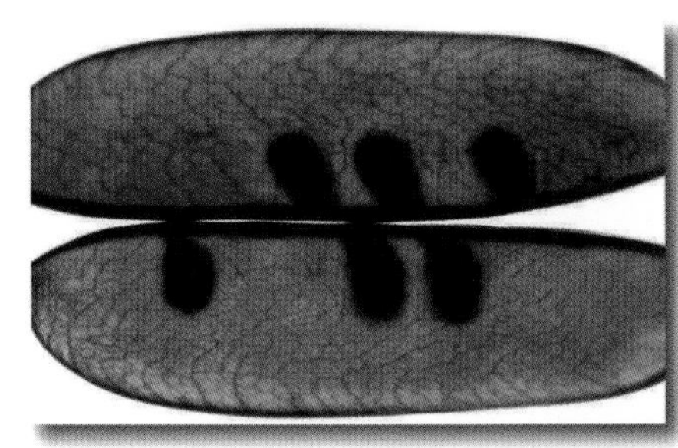

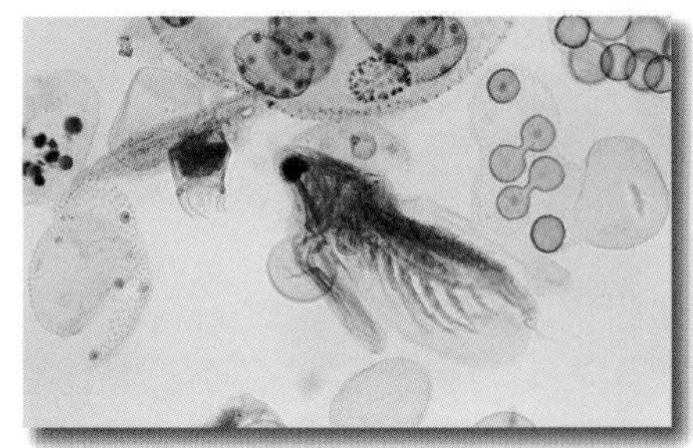
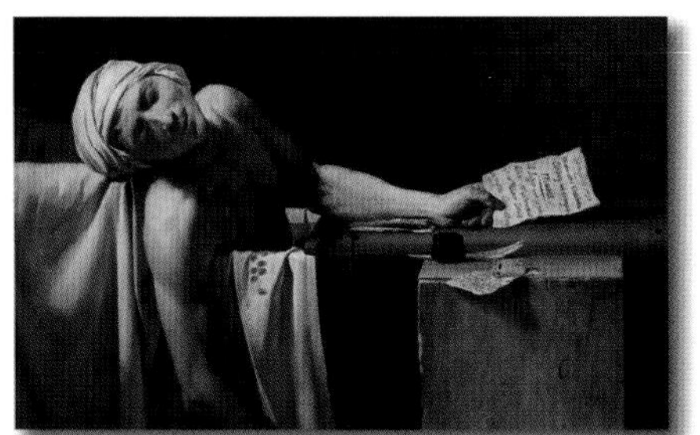

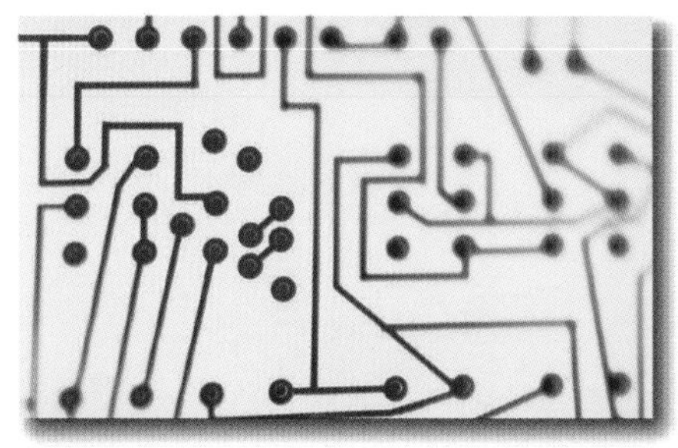
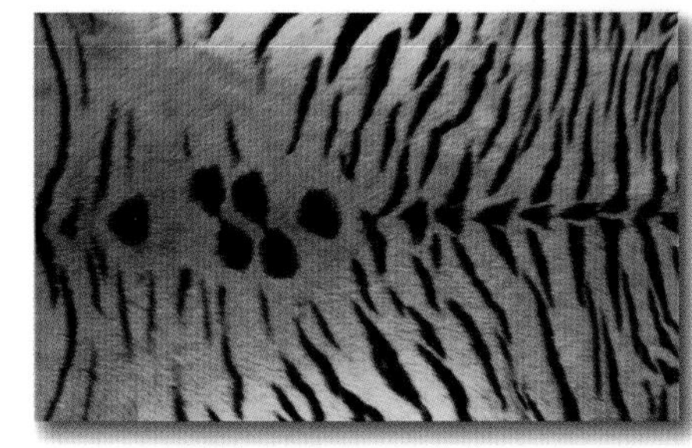

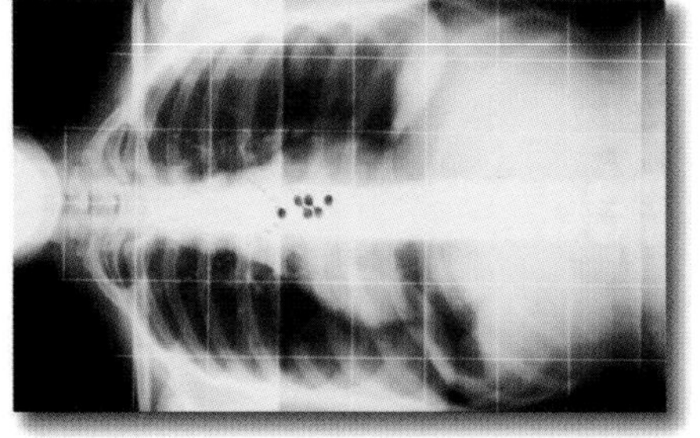

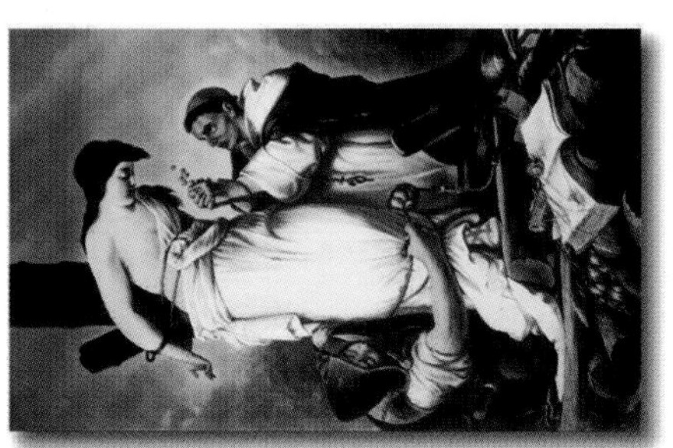
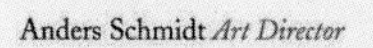

(this spread) Design Firm **Intellecta Corporate** Art Director **Anders Schmidt** Client **Intellecta**

INTELLECTA CORPORATE
Box 45045, Sveavägen 53, SE-104 30 Stockholm, Sweden
Tel: +46.8.729 96 00, Fax: +46.8.729 96 05
www.intellectacorporate.se

Intellecta Corporate AB is a part of the Intellecta Group.
Registered in Stockholm. CORP. ID NO. [illegible] VAT NO. [illegible]

Anders Schmidt *Art Director*

INTELLECTA CORPORATE
Sveavägen 53, Box 45045, SE-104 30 Stockholm
Tel: +46.8.729 96 00. Dir: +46.8.729 96 27. Cell: +46.709.75 99 26
Fax: +46.8.729 96 65. e-mail: anders.schmidt@intellecta.se

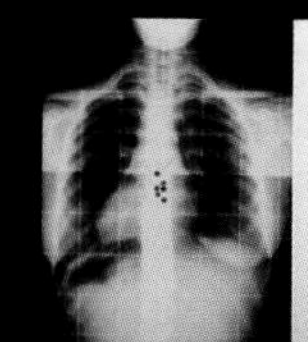

INTELLECTA CORPORATE
Sveavägen 53, Box 45045, SE-104 30 Stockholm, Sweden

GENUINE
QUALCOMM
ACCESSORIES

QUALCOMM
QUALCOMM
Q PHONE REFERENCE GUIDE
QUALCOMM
QUALCOMM
Q PHONE INTERACTIVE TRAINING CD-ROM
Q PHONE INTERACTIVE TRAINING CD-ROM
1900 MHz
CDMA Digital PCS Phone
the power of
QUALCOMM
CLEAR CALLS. PRIVATE. SECURE.

QUALCOMM
CDMA DIGITAL/ANALOG CELLULAR PHONE
QCP-820
DUAL MODE
QUALCOMM
CDMA DIGITAL PCS & ANALOG CELLULAR PHONE
QCP-2700
DUAL BAND DUAL MODE
QUALCOMM
CDMA DIGITAL PCS WIRELESS PHONE
QCP-1920
Wireless Phone
Wireless Phone
Wireless Phone
Every word from your mouth will be secure and private.
Crisp, clear calls. How's that sound?

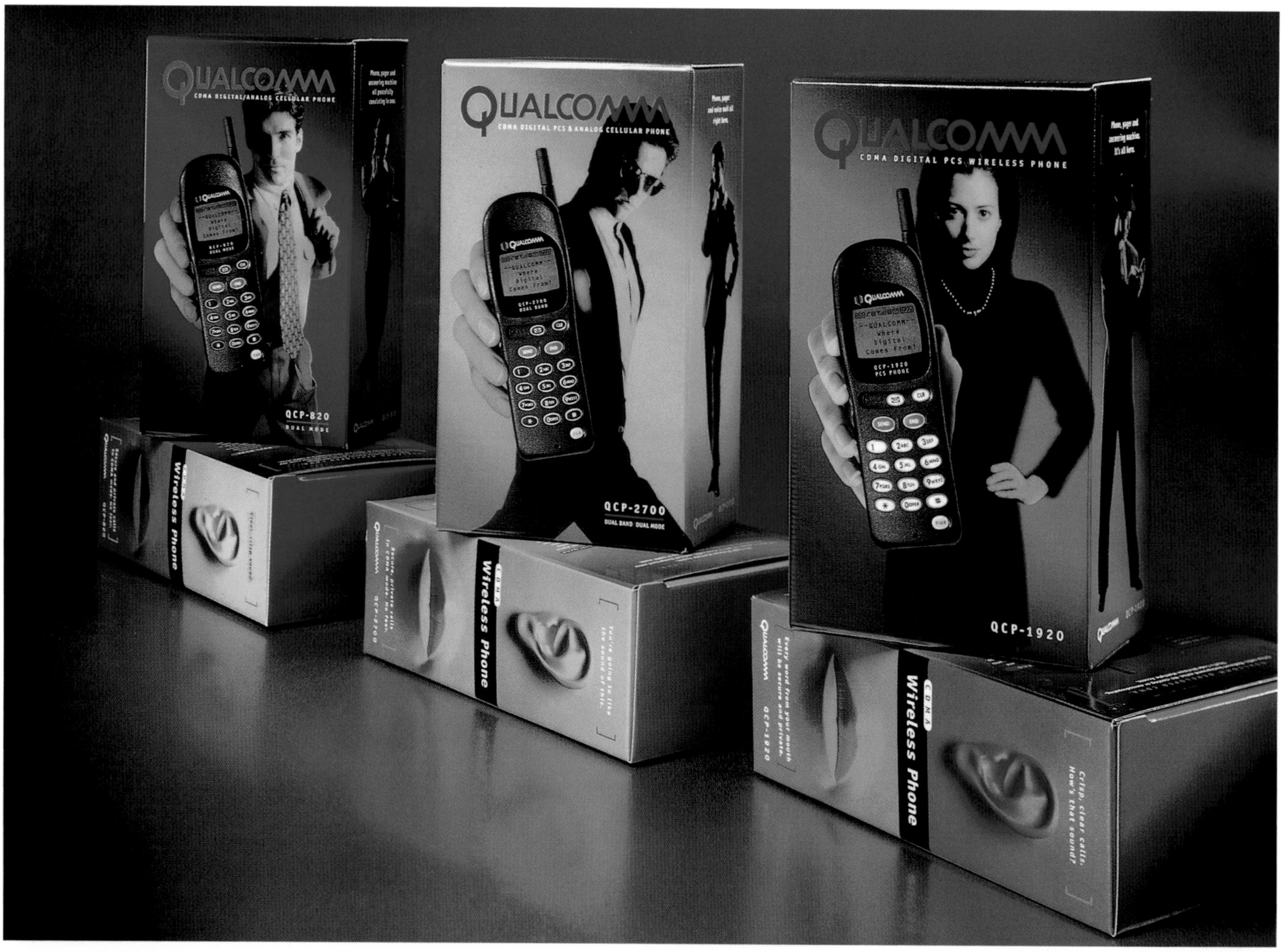

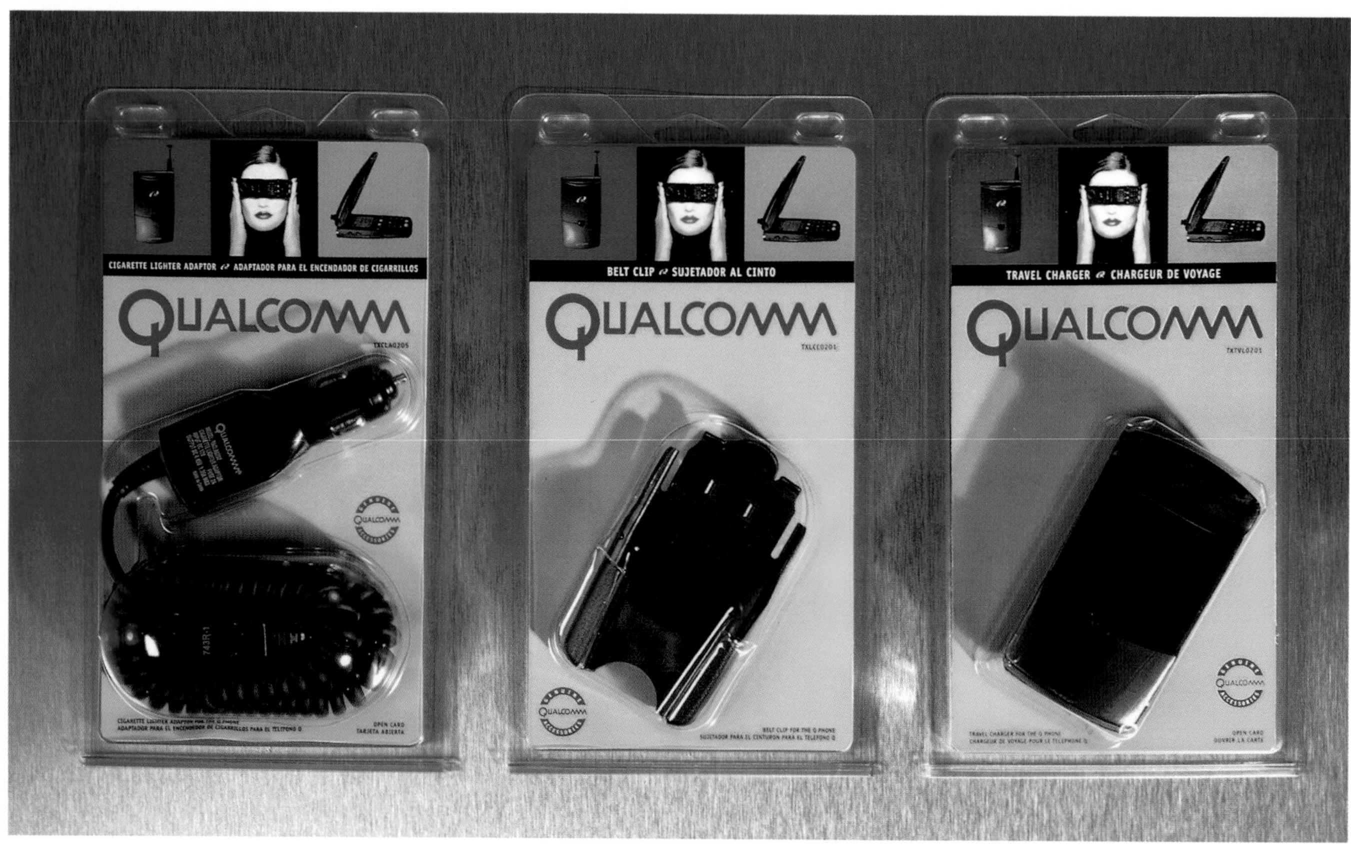

CIGARETTE LIGHTER ADAPTOR ADAPTADOR PARA EL ENCENDADOR DE CIGARRILLOS
QUALCOMM
BELT CLIP SUJETADOR AL CINTO
QUALCOMM
TRAVEL CHARGER CHARGEUR DE VOYAGE
QUALCOMM

QUALCOMM
QUALCOMM
pdQ
1900 MHz
QUALCOMM

QUALCOMM
CDMA PCS PHONE • TELEPHONE CDMA PCS • TELEFONO CDMA PCS
1900 MHz
PRIVACY
PRIVACIDAD
It's (1) a phone, (2) a pager and (3) voice mail.

QUALCOMM
QUALCOMM
CDMA PCS PHONE
Q PHONE INTERACTIVE TRAINING CD-ROM

QUALCOMM
QUALCOMM
QUALCOMM
QCP-860
QUALCOMM

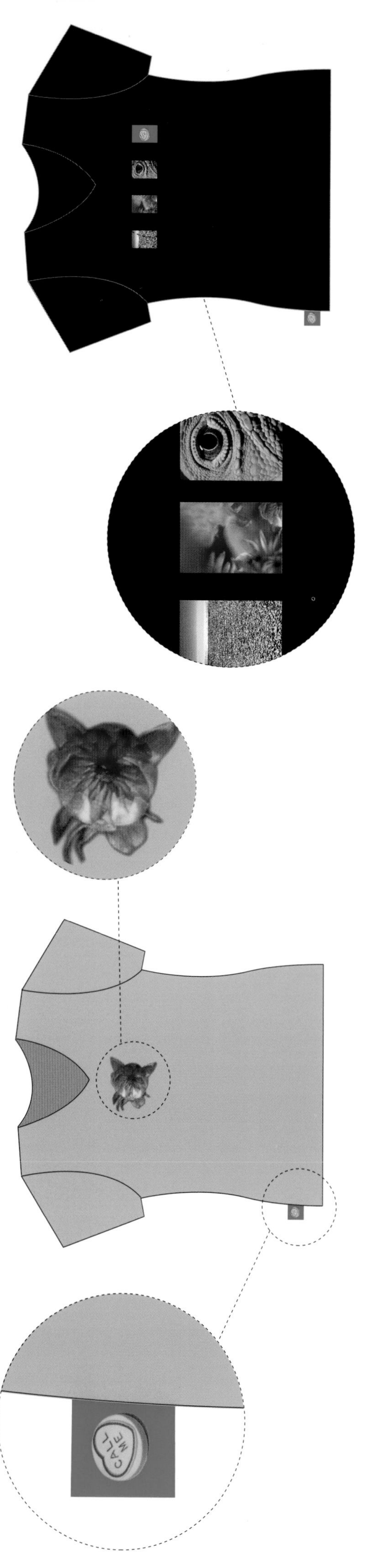
CALL ME

(this spread) Design Firm **DNA Design Ltd.** Creative Director **Grenville Main** Art Directors & Designers **Sarah Laing** and **Charlie Ward** Illustrators **Sarah Laing** and **Caro Cole** Copywriters **Gary O'Neill** and **Andrew Gair** Client **Telecom New Zealand** Communications 44,45 (this spread) Design Firm **Beacon Communications K. K.** Creative Director **Alejandro M. Lopez** Art Director **Mayumi Kato** Designers **Chie Arakawa, Misako Maruyama, Akiko Tanaka, Mizuki Matsuda** and **Yukiko Kamematsu** Client **Beacon Communications K. K.**

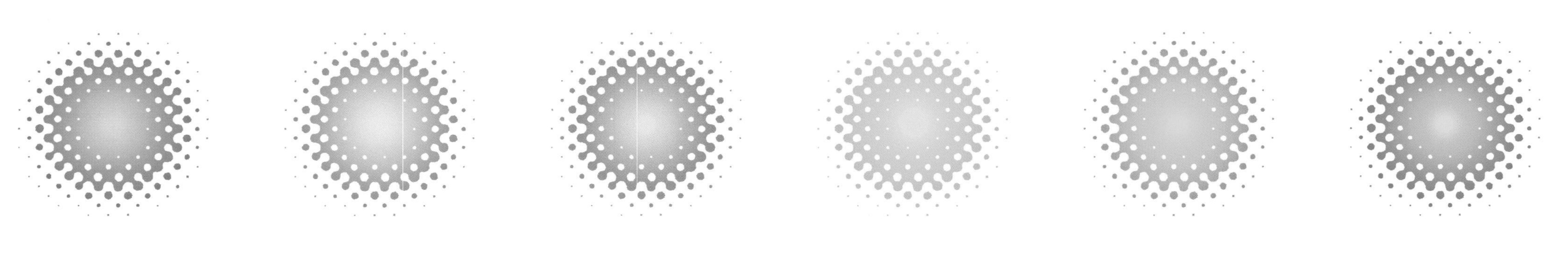

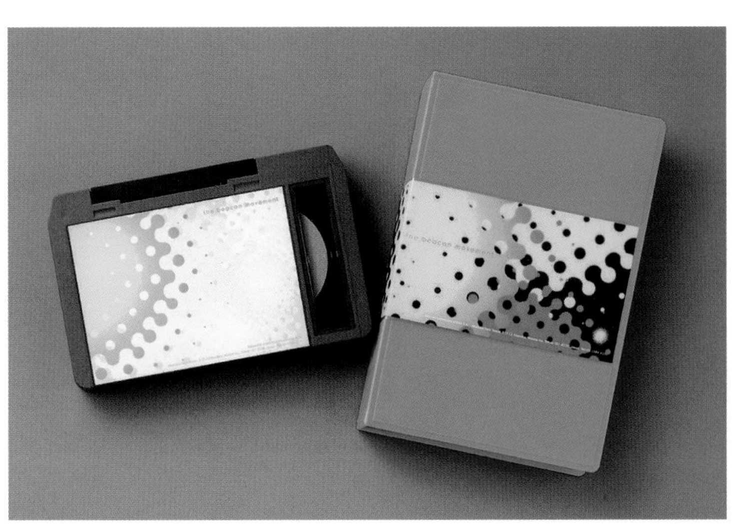

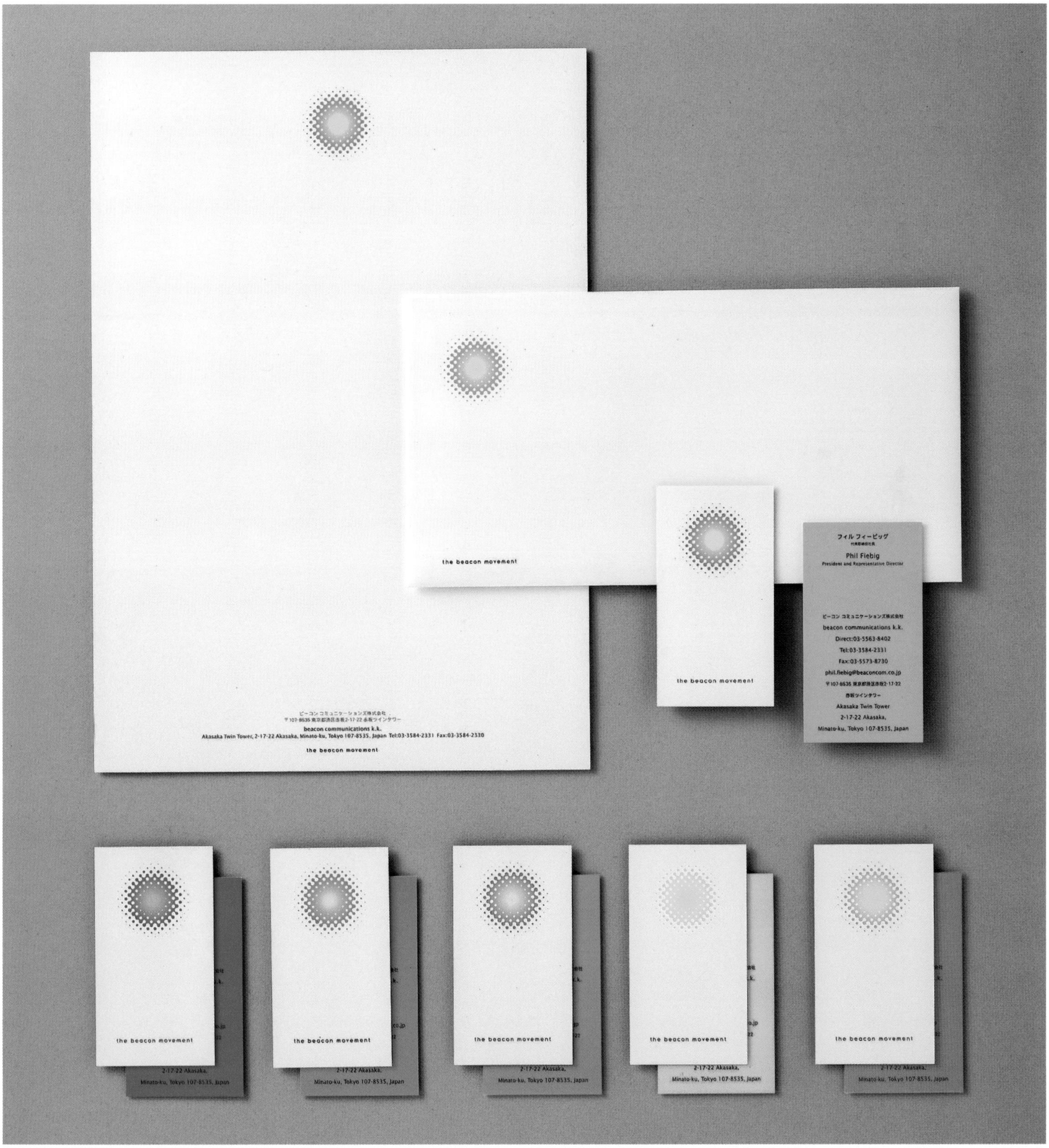

ビーコン コミュニケーションズ株式会社
〒107-8535 東京都港区赤坂2-17-22 赤坂ツインタワー
beacon communications k.k.
Akasaka Twin Tower, 2-17-22 Akasaka, Minato-ku, Tokyo 107-8535, Japan Tel:03-3584-2331 Fax:03-3584-2330
the beacon movement

the beacon movement

the beacon movement

フィル フィービッグ
Phil Fiebig
President and Representative Director
ビーコン コミュニケーションズ株式会社
beacon communications k.k.
Direct:03-5563-8402
Tel:03-3584-2331
Fax:03-5573-8730
phil.fiebig@beaconcom.co.jp
赤坂ツインタワー
Akasaka Twin Tower
2-17-22 Akasaka,
Minato-ku, Tokyo 107-8535, Japan

the beacon movement

the beacon movement

the beacon movement

the beacon movement

the beacon movement

(this spread) Design Firm **Cornwell Design** Creative Director, Art Director and Copywriter **Steven Cornwell** Designer and Illustrator **Tim Sutherland** Photographer **Lynton Crabb** Client **Eye Corp**

eye CORP
visual energy
eyedentical
eye

eye CORP
visual energy
bullseye

eye CORP
visual energy
eye
multipleye

(this spread) Design Firm **TAXI** Creative Director **Jane Hope** Designers **Daniel Andreani, Natalie Cusson** and **Michael Lapointe** Photographer **Shin Sugino** Copywriters **Peter Ignazi** and **Hagen Ainsworth** Client **Clearnet**

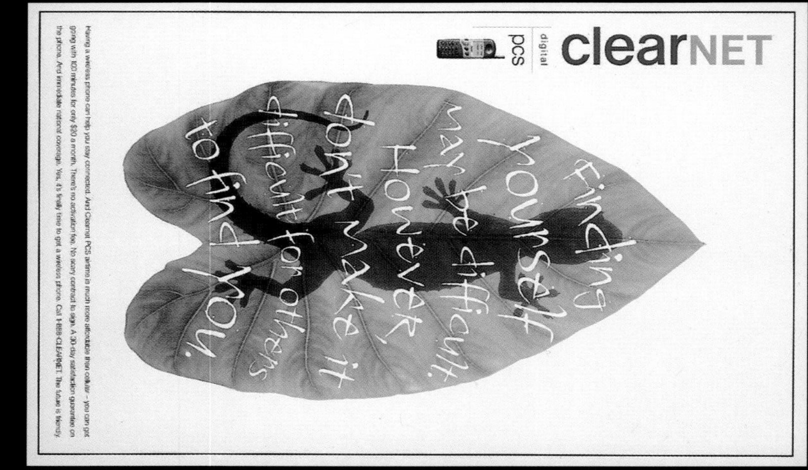

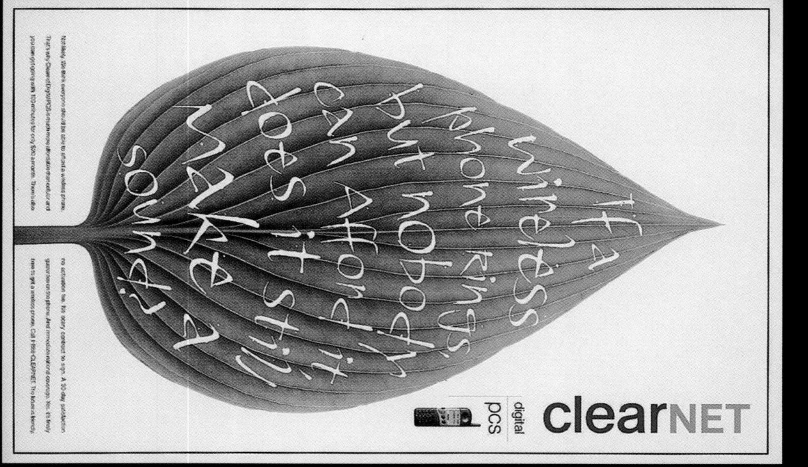

clearNET
digital
pcs
CLEARNET-PCS
clearNET
clearNET
digital
pcs
CLEARNET-PCS

(this spread) Design Firm **Turner Duckworth** Creative Directors **David Turner** and **Bruce Duckworth** Designers **David Turner** and **Jonathan Warner** Photographers **Michael Lamotte** and **Martin Scholler** Client **Palm Inc.**

PALM BRAND IDENTITY
HANDLE
WITH CARE
Match Chips
palm

palm

palm
Vx
Handheld
Ultra Slim
Travel light. Travel smart. Add more applications.
palm
IIIc
Handheld
Color & Clarity
Visualize your world in color.
palm
VIIx
Handheld
Wireless Internet
Instantly access the Internet, e-mail and messaging.

(this spread) Design Firm **Girvin, Inc.** Creative Director **Jeff Haack** Designers **Jeff Lancaster** and **Laurie Vette** Photographer **Steve Keating** Copywriter **Deborah Ashin** Client **Microsoft**

The history of a revolutionary idea that helped
Before 1975
The PC revolution begins
mid-1970's
PC's take off
The 1980's
The Windows Era
The Early 1990's
Microsoft debuts
Providing the platform
Opening new windows
1985

EXIT

Shiel Sexton

spread) Design Firm **Young and Laramore** Executive Creative Directors **David Young** and **Jeff Laramore** Creative Director **Carolyn Hadlock** Art Director **Matt Ganser** Photographer **Tod Martens** Designer and Illustrator **David Bellamy** Copywriter **Carrie Voorhis** Client

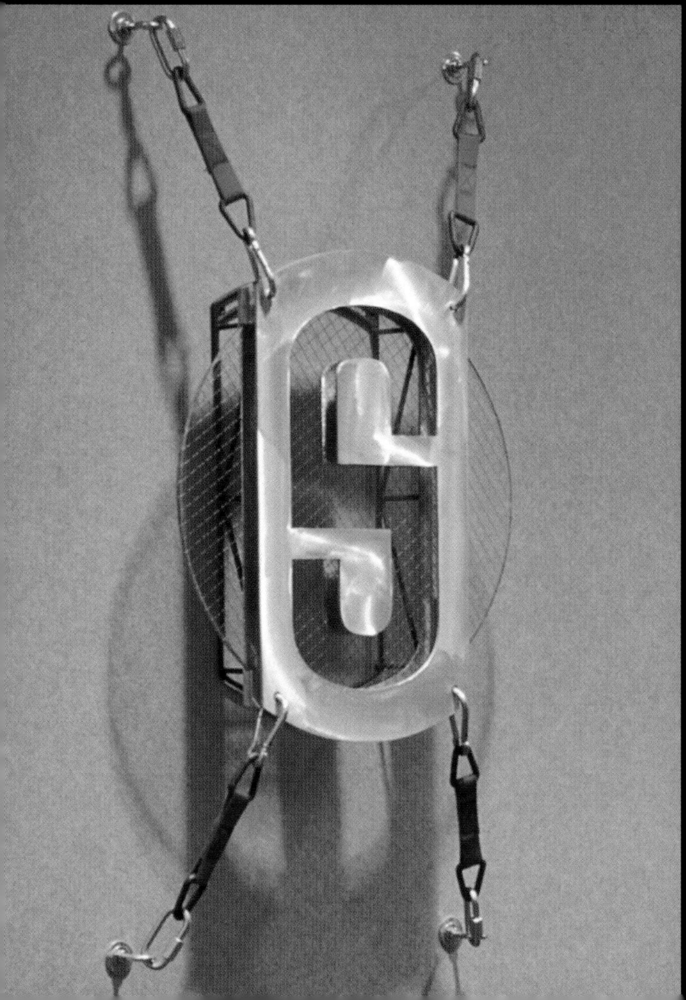

owing spread) Design Firm **Marksimovic & Partners** Creative Director **Ivica Maksimovic** Art Directors **Rita Thinnes, Patrick Bittneri** and **Sabine Wilhelm** Photographer **André Mailander** Copywriter **Germaine Paulus** Client **Dittgen Bauuntern**

› Datum:

› Thema/Projekt:

› Ort:

› Zeit:

› Teilnehmer:

› Inhalt

unternehmen GmbH

Saarbrücker Straße 99 | 66839 Schmelz | Postfach 1027 | 66832 Schmelz | Telefon 06887/307-0 Telefax 06887/307-199 | www.dittgen.de | e-mail: info@dittgen.de

anwesenheit

(Fin P27)

› Ausbildungsbetreuer: Stefan Neumeyer 06887/307-282

› Auszubildender:

› Personal-Nummer:

› Ausbildungsjahr: 1 2 3

› Berufsschule:

› KW	‹ Montag	‹ Dienstag	‹ Mittwoch	‹ Donnerstag	‹ Freitag	‹ Samstag
› Datum:						
› Beginn:						
› Ende:						
› Stunden:						
› Bezeichnung						

K	krank			B	Betrieb
U	Urlaub	F	früher gegangen	S	Schule
FE	fehlt entschuldigt	V	Verspätung	A	Ausbildungzentrum
FU	fehlt unentschuldigt	Fei	Feiertag	iU	innerbetrieblicher Unterricht

› Schafbrücke, den › Ausbildungsmeister

› Saarlouis/Neunkirchen, den › Berufsschullehrer

› Schmelz, den › Auszubildender

› Schmelz, den › gesehen: Ausbildungsbetreuer

Bauunternehmen GmbH

dittgen

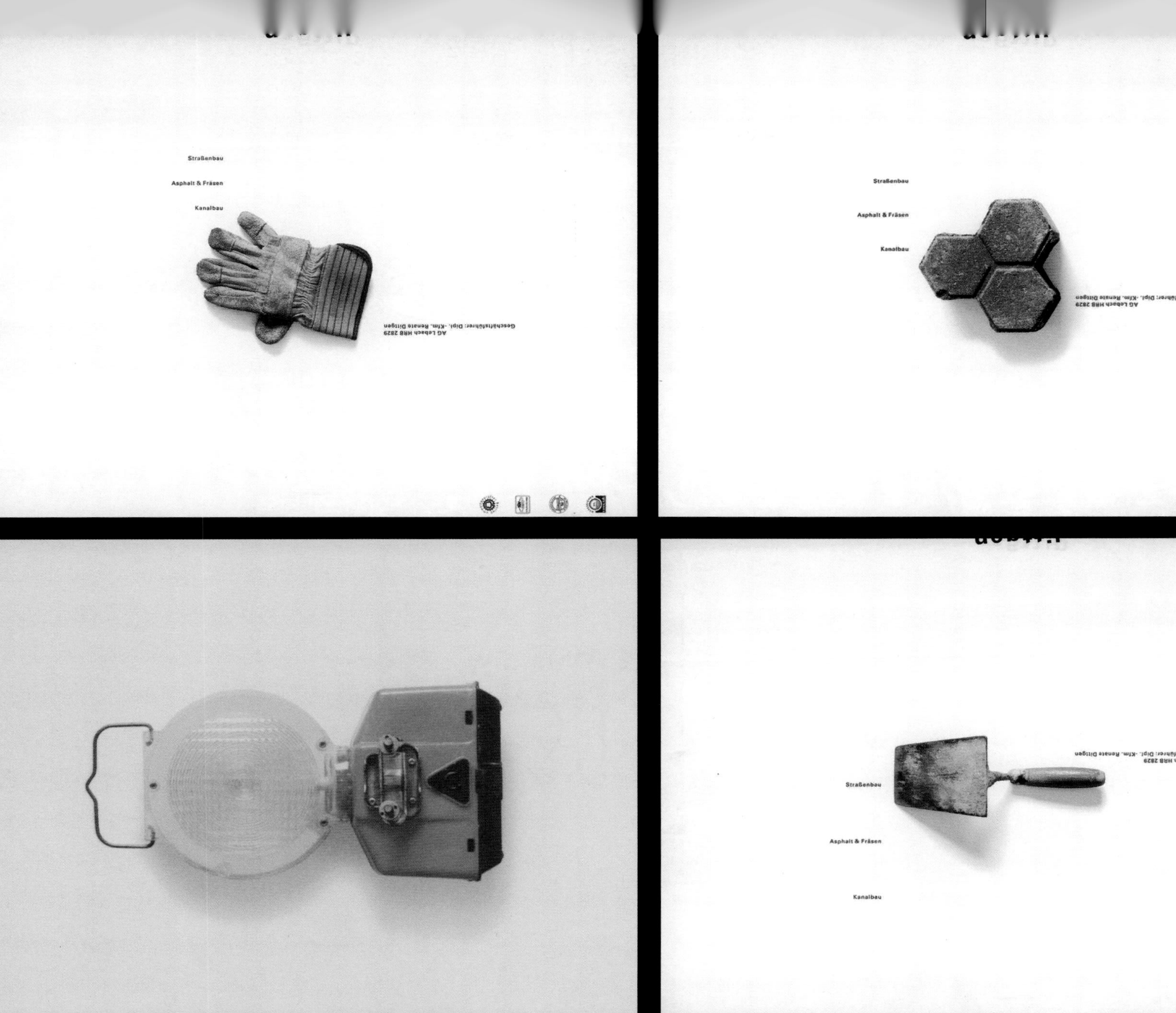
Straßenbau
Asphalt & Fräsen
Kanalbau
AG Lebach HRB 2829
Geschäftsführer: Dipl.-Kfm. Renate Diltgen
Straßenbau
Asphalt & Fräsen
Kanalbau
AG Lebach HRB 2829
Geschäftsführer: Dipl.-Kfm. Renate Diltgen
Straßenbau
Asphalt & Fräsen
Kanalbau
AG Lebach HRB 2829
Geschäftsführer: Dipl.-Kfm. Renate Diltgen

MISSION
TUSCAN · ANTIQUE SAHARA · BUFFSTONE BELLA
When looks matter and craftsmanship counts.
MADE IN AMERICA
DELEO CLAY TILE COMPANY · 600 CHANEY STREET, LAKE ELSINORE, CALIFORNIA 92530 · WWW.DELEOCLAYTILE.COM

Mires Design Creative and Art Director **José A. Serrano** Designers **Miguel Perez, Gale Spitzley, Deborah Hom** and **David Adey** Client **Deleo Clay Tile Company**

DELEO CLAY TILE COMPANY
MANUFACTURERS OF THROUGHBODY TILES
DELEO CLAY
TILE COMPANY

MANUFACTURERS OF QUALITY
DELEO CLAY TILE CO.
DELEO CLAY TILE CO

DELEO CLAY TILE
COMPANY

MANUFACTURERS OF QUALITY
Trade
Mark
DELEO CLAY TILE CO.
MADE IN THE USA
EST. 1984
THROUGHBODY CLAY TILES

Willis E. Hartshorn
Director
International Center of Photography
1133 Avenue of the Americas New York NY 10036
T 212 860 1777 F 212 768 4688 www.icp.org
whartshorn@icp.org

Firm **Siegelgale** Creative Director **Vanessa Ryan** Art Director **Kenneth Cooke** Designers **Glennys Anglada** and **Chuanda Tan** Client **ICP (Interantional Center of Photography)**

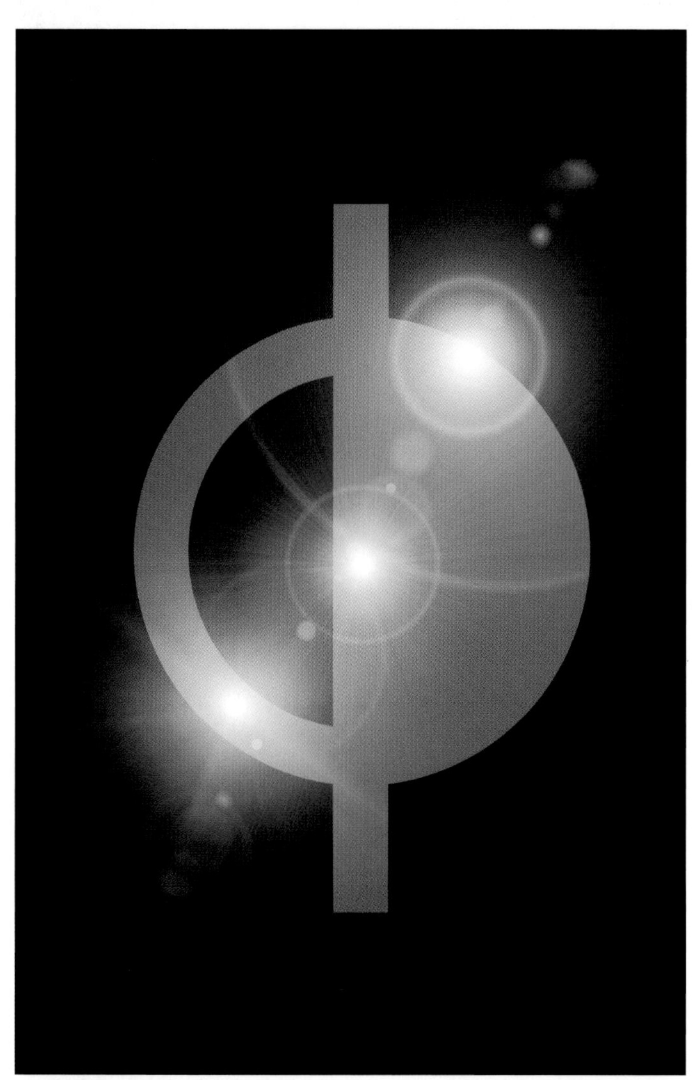

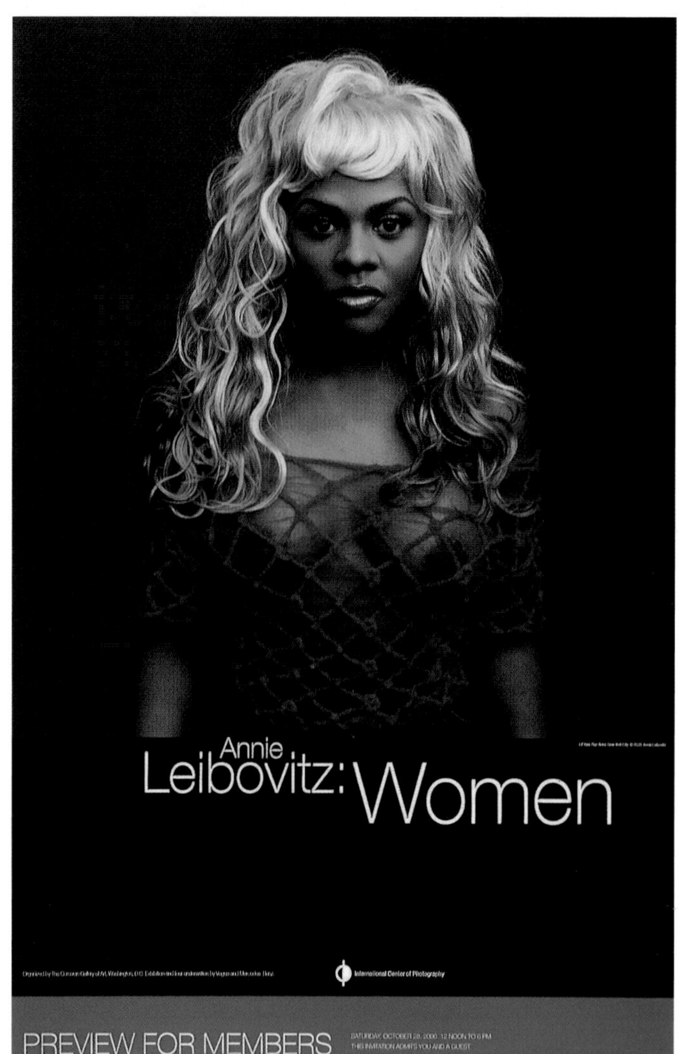
Annie
Leibovitz: Women
International Center of Photography
PREVIEW FOR MEMBERS
THIS INVITATION ADMITS YOU AND A GUEST

Reflections in a Glass Eye: Works from the International Center of Photography Collection
International Center of Photography

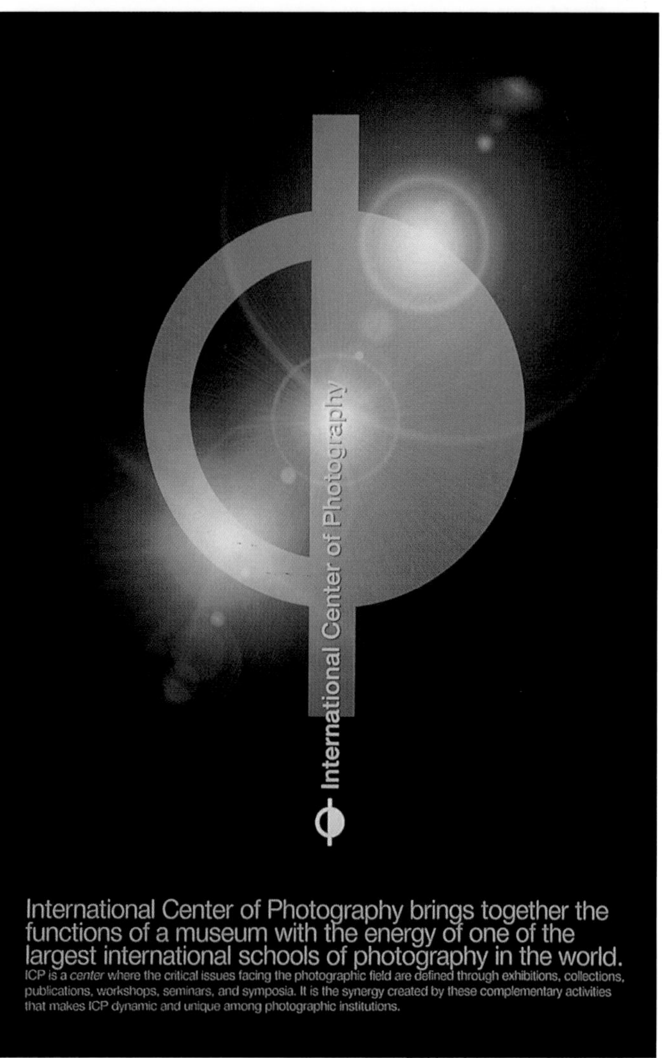
International Center of Photography
International Center of Photography brings together the functions of a museum with the energy of one of the largest international schools of photography in the world.
ICP is a *center* where the critical issues facing the photographic field are defined through exhibitions, collections, publications, workshops, seminars, and symposia. It is the synergy created by these complementary activities that makes ICP dynamic and unique among photographic institutions.

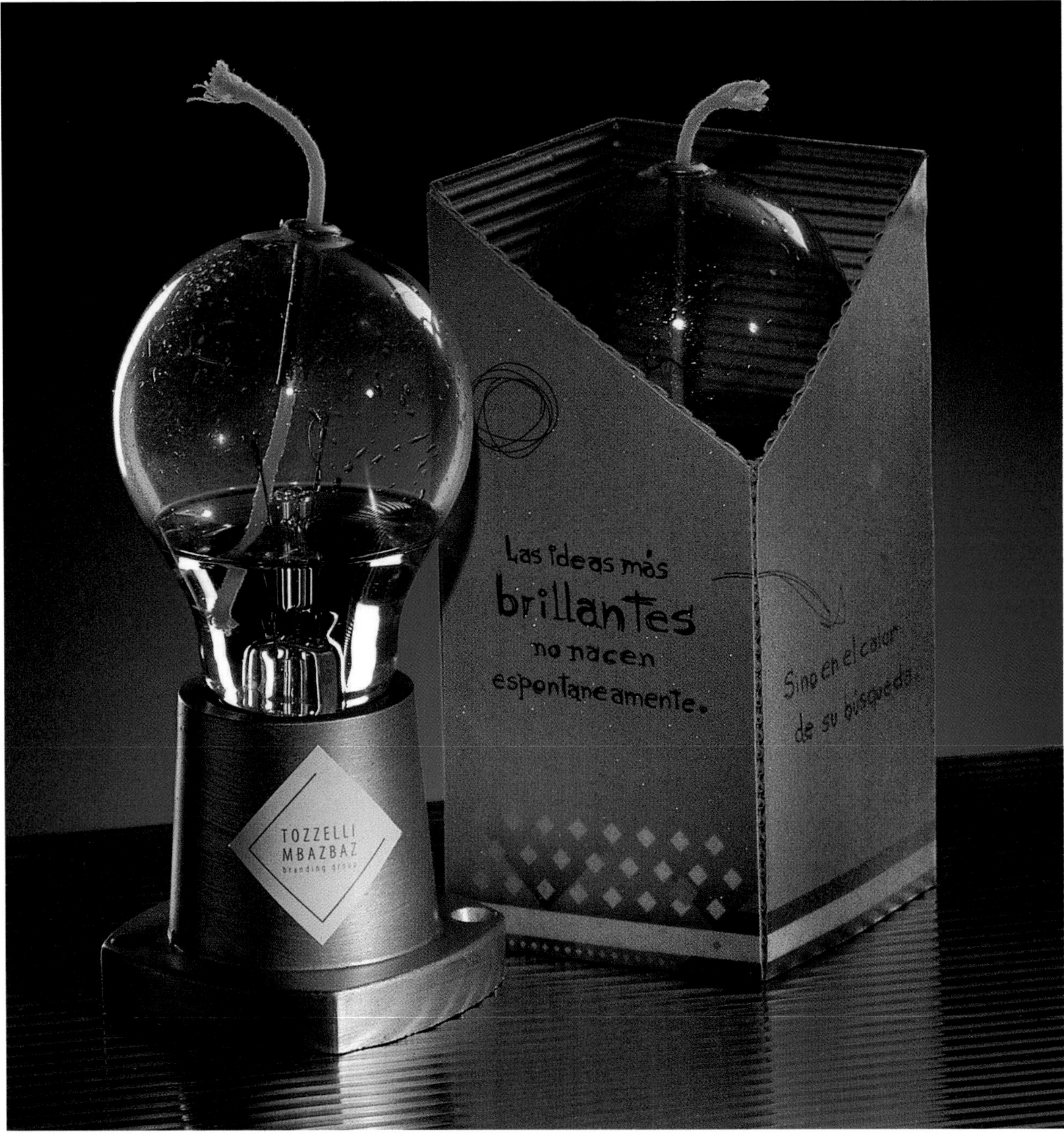
TOZZELLI
MBAZBAZ
branding group
Las ideas más
brillantes
no nacen
espontaneamente.
Sino en el calor
de su búsqueda.

(this spread) Design Firm **Tozzelli-Mbazbaz** Creative Directors **Vanesa Tozzelli** and **Laura Mbazbaz** Art Director **Laura Mbazbaz** Designer and Illustrator **Valeria Rodriguez do Campo** Client **Tozzelli-Mbazbaz**

TOZZELLI MBAZBAZ
TOZZELLI
MBAZBAZ
Vanesa Tozzelli
TOZZELLI
MBAZBAZ

(this spread) Design Firm **Deep Design** Creative Director **Rick Grimsley** Designers **Mark Steingruber** and **Rick Grimsley** Illustrator **Mark Steingruber** Client **United Parcel Service**

PANDA EXPRESS
ups

United Parcel Service
UPS PANDA EXPRESS
BEIJING • ATLANTA
PANDA EXPRESS
315

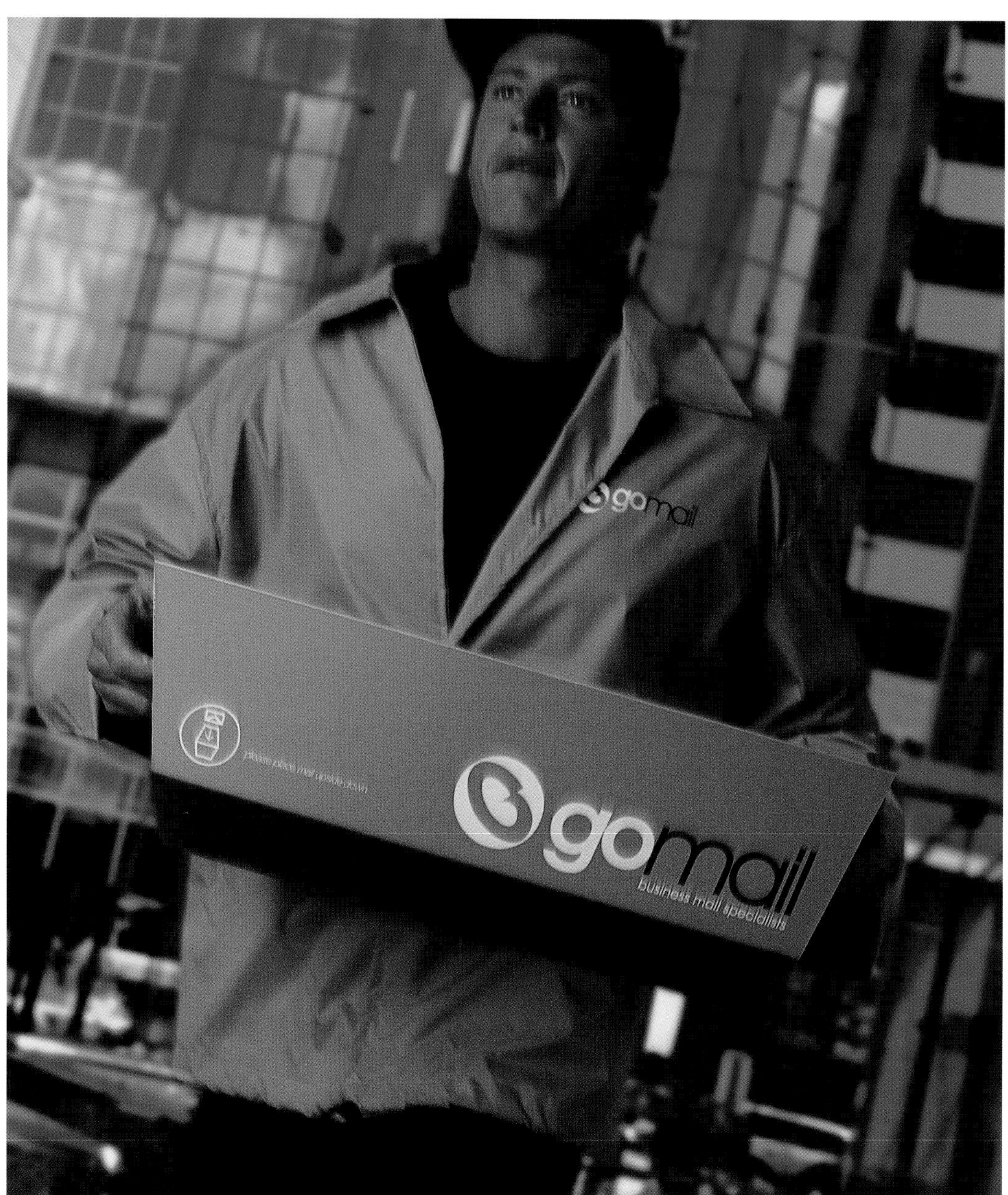

(this spread) Design Firm **Cornwell Design** Creative Director **Steven Cornwell** Client **Ausdoc Group**

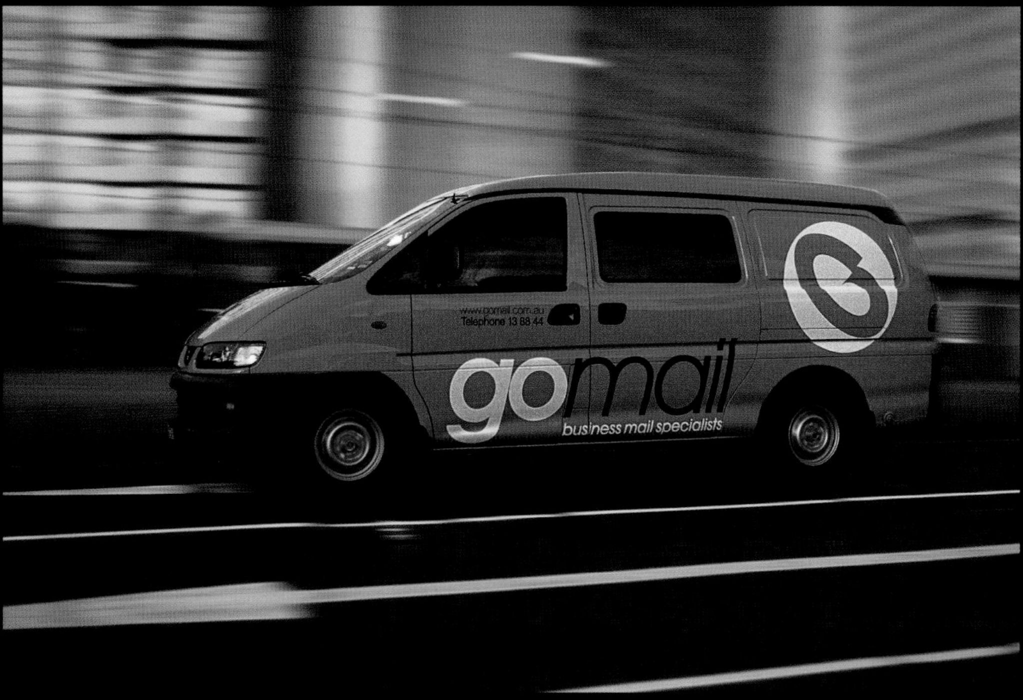

gomail
business mail specialists
go
gomail
business mail specialists
go

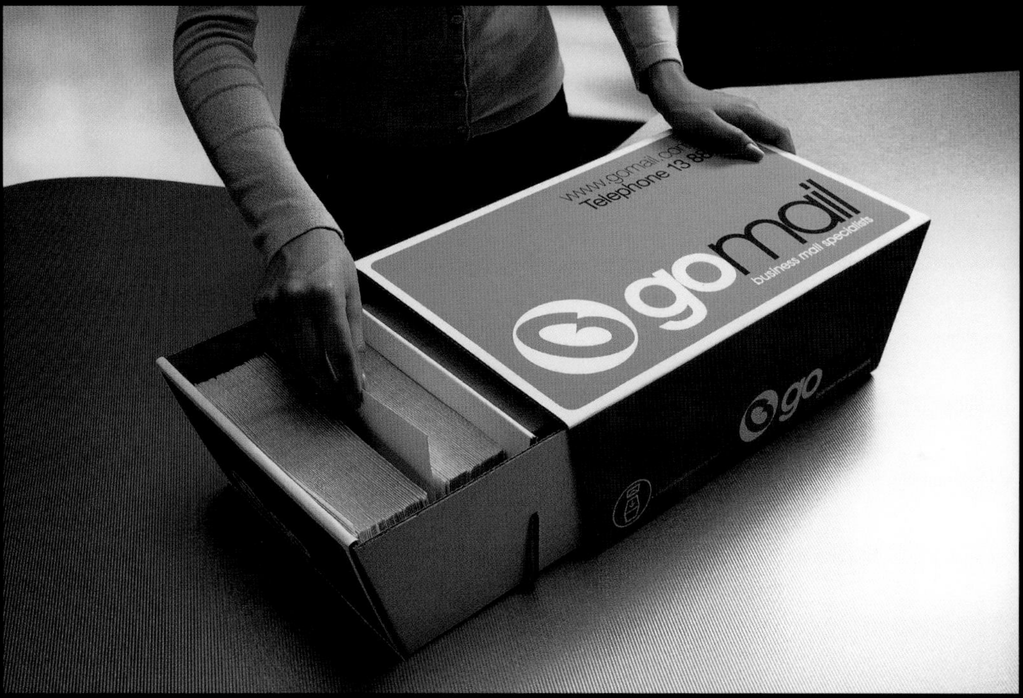

(this spread) Design Firm **ZIBA Design** Creative Director **Sohrab Vossoughi** Designers **Elaine Bothe, Chelsea Vandiver** and **Omer Kotzer** Architect **Randy Poulsen** Copywriter **Bob Sweet** Client **FedEx**

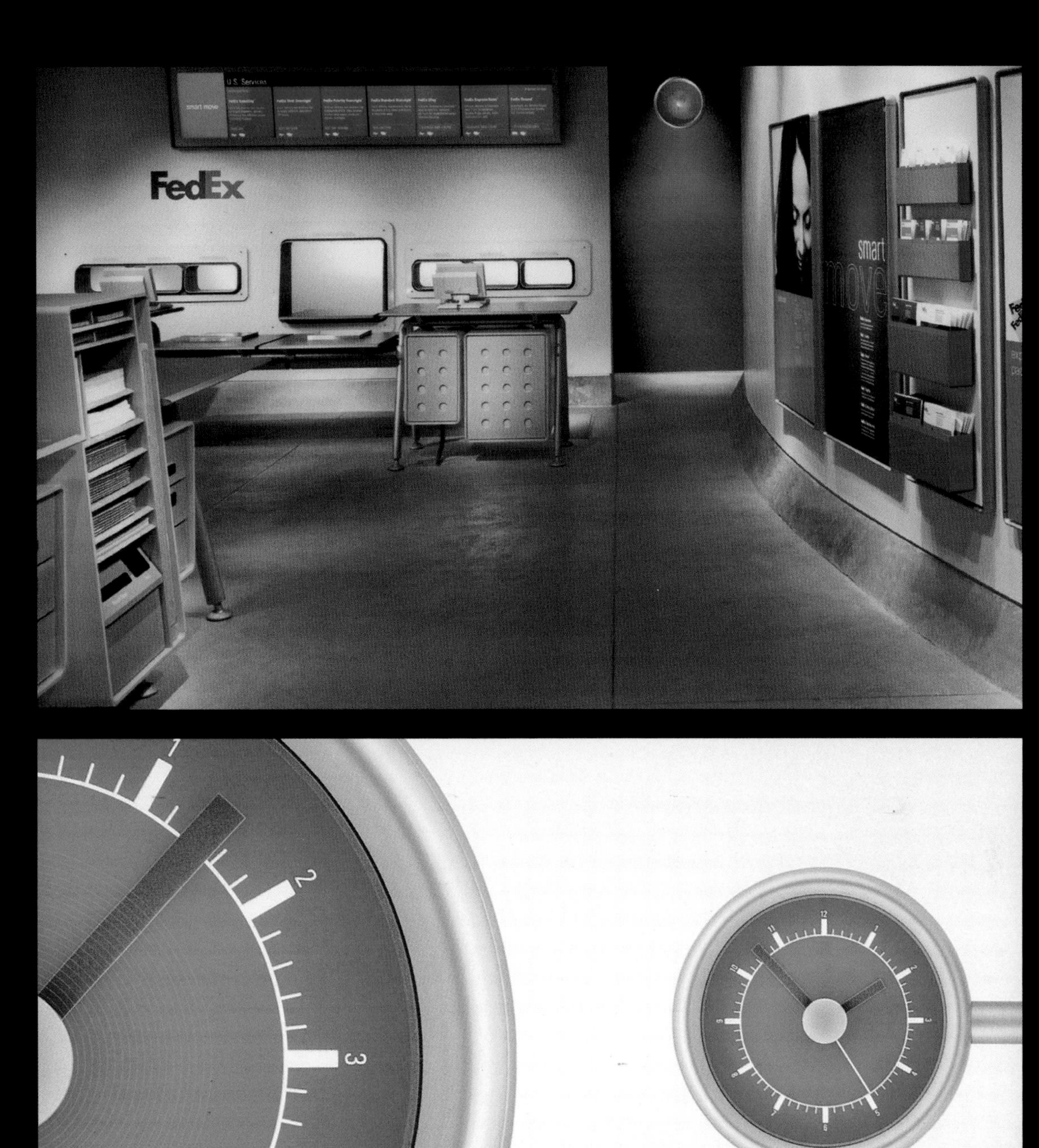
FedEx
smart
move

(this spread) Design Firm **Pentagram Design** Designers **Michael Gerricke, Su Matthews** and **Maggie West** Architects **James Biber, Michael Zweck-Bronner** and **Jim Cleary** Photographer **Andrew Bordwin** Client **UPS World Services Store**

ON TIME,
or we'll refund your shipping charges.
IT'S ON US
OVER THERE,
We guarantee overnight delivery to
THE WORLD

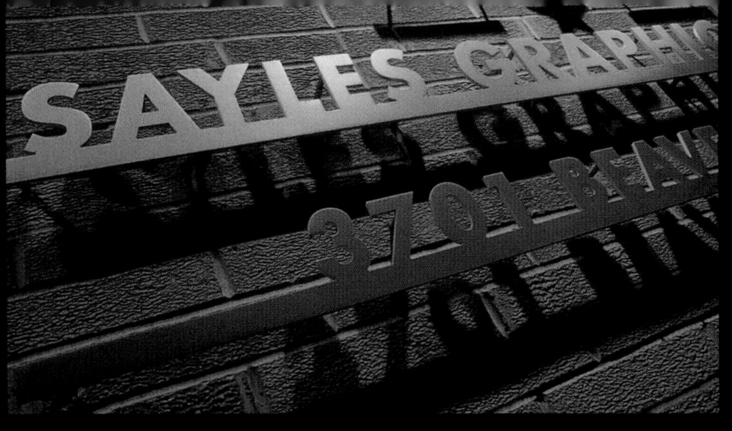

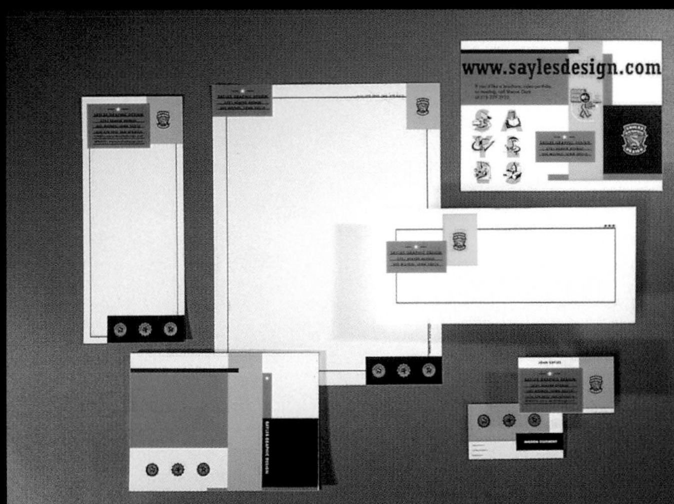

Firm **Sayles Graphic Design** Creative Director, Art Director, Designer and Illustrator **John Sayles** Photographer **Bill Nellans** Copywriter **Kristin Mafra** Client **Sayles Graphic Design**

SAYLES GRAPHIC DESIGN
15 YEARS
TIME FLIES
1985
2000
FIFTEEN YEARS
PARTNERS
TIME FLIES.
But you can keep track of it with our special "birthday" gift to you. It's our way of saying THANKS for 15 years of friendship and good times.
This limited edition watch is signed and numbered by John Sayles!

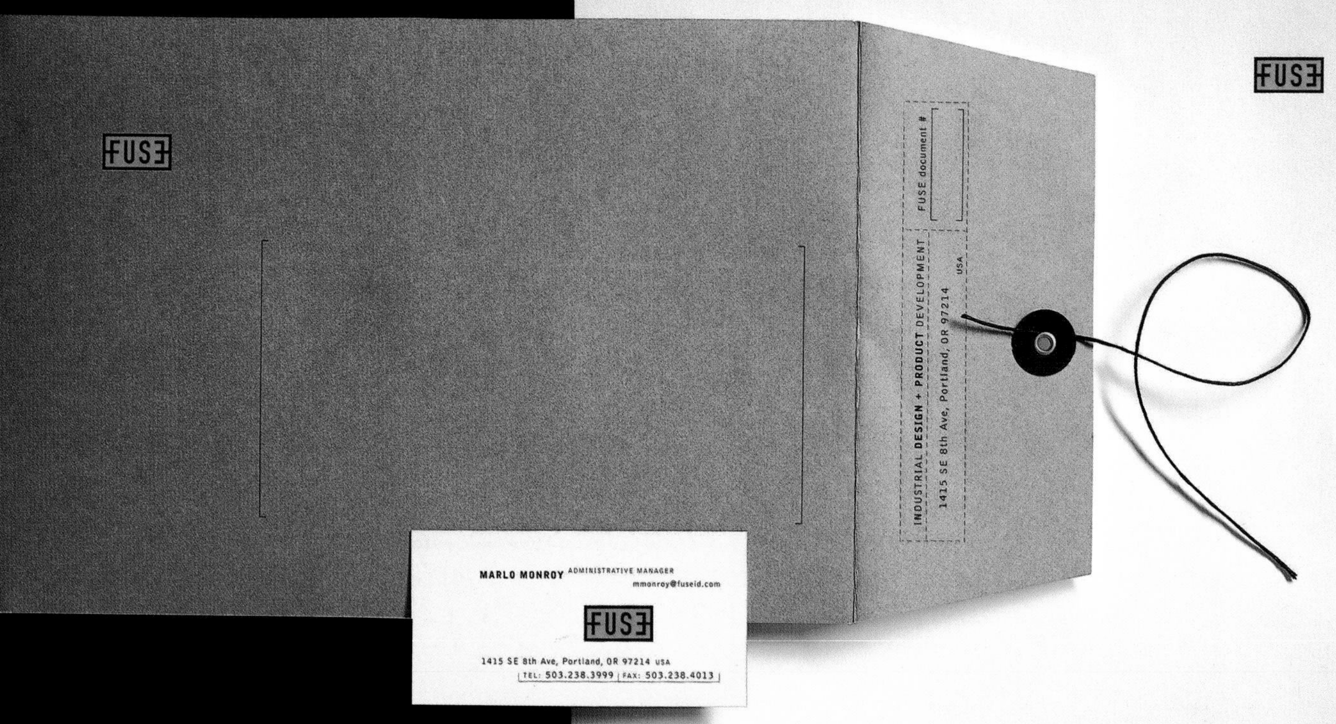

Design Firm **Sandstrom Design** Creative Director, Art Director, Designer and Copywriter **Steve Sandstrom** Production Designer **Sarah Cooke** Client **Fuse**

Design Firm **Wallace Church, Inc.** Creative Director **Stan Church** Art Director **Nin Glaister** Designer **Lawrence Haggerty** Photographer **Markus Hewitt** Client **Wallace Church, Inc.**

(this spread) Design Firm **Pentagram Design** Art Director **Michael Bierut** Designers **Michael Bierut** and **Jackqueline Thaw** Client **Fashion Institute of Technology**

Fashion Institute of Technology, New York (212)217-7675 www.fitnyc.suny.edu

BFA in Toy Design

If you have talent, the magic of childhood in your heart, and the desire to work toward a creative and rewarding career, FIT's Bachelor of Fine Arts program in Toy Design is for you.

More than ever, the toy industry needs great designers: professionals who create children's products that are safe, fun, and challenge the imagination. Working with the support of the Toy Manufacturers of America, FIT has developed a program that will fully prepare you for a career in the toy industry.

How successful is the program? Ninety-five percent of Toy Design graduates have been places in jobs at major toy companies and inventor groups.

F.I.T., located in the heart of Manhattan, is a specialized college of the State University of New York. Limited tuition assistance and housing are available.

For early consideration, call or write to:
Judy Ellis
Toy Design Department
Room B231
Fashion Institute of Technology
Seventh Avenue at 27 Street
New York City 10001-5992
212/760-7133

FIT is play

Educational opportunities at F.I.T. are offered without regard to age, gender, race, color, religion, national origin, sexual orientation, marital status, disability, or veteran status.

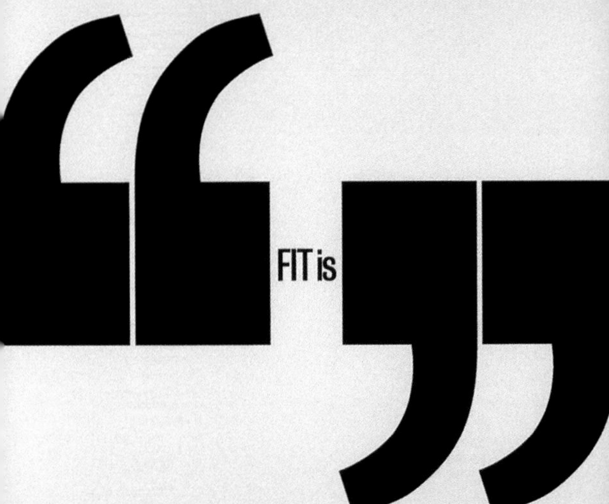

technology
digital
New York
looking
radical
FIT is
fashion
24
uptown
ideas
cosmopolitan
tomorrow
design
beauty
urban
modern
international
moving
happening
advertising
here
loud
downtown

(this spread) Design Firm **Sussman/Prejza & Co., Inc.** Creative Director **Deborah Sussman** Art Director and Designer **John Johnston** Photographers **Jim Simmons, Annette Del Zoppo** and **Everett & Soule** Client **Universal Creative, Orlando Florida**

CINEPLEX
UNIVER
LOEWS
THEATRES

EVEREST
SOUTHWEST AIRLINES
THE LIVING SEA
Now Showing!
FOX 6
WBRC
94.5
The Birmingham News
Birmingham Post-Herald
IMAX
DOME
THEATER
McWANE CENTER
ADVENTURES IN SCIENCE

(this spread) Design Firm **Lorenc & Yoo Design** Creative and Art Director **Jan Lorenc** Designers **Steve McCall, David Park, Chung Youl Yoo** and **Veda Sammy** Photographer **Rion Rizzo** Illustrators **Michelle Scott** and **Veda Sammy** Client **McWane Center - John MacKay** (this spread) Agency **Sussman/Prejza & Co., Inc.** Creative Director **Scott Cuyler** Art Director **Deborah Sussman** Designer **Holly Hampton** Photographer **Jim Simmons/Annette del Zoppo Prod.** Client **New Jersey Performing Arts Center**

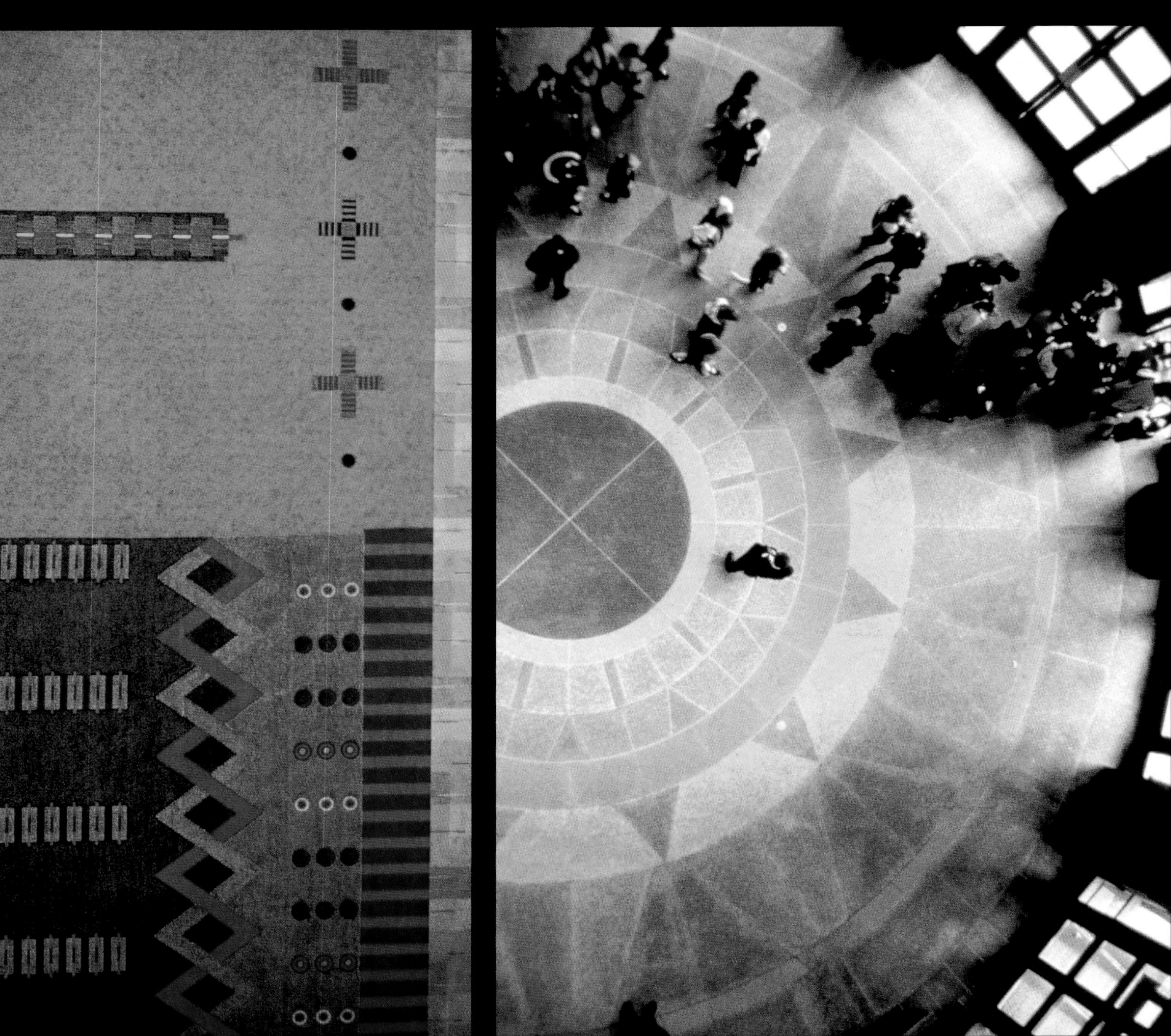

Second Tier
Seats 101-126

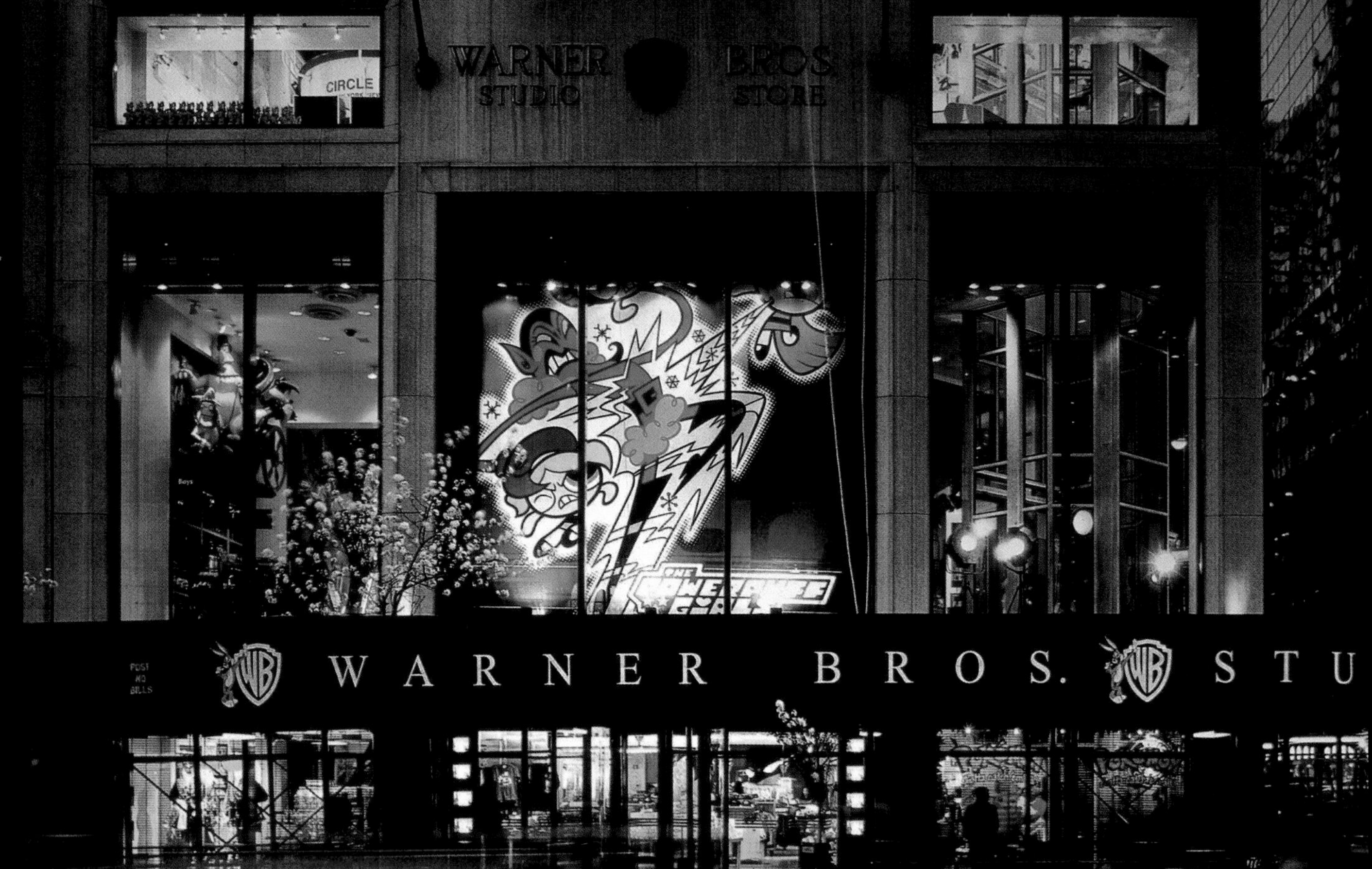

Cartoon Network Art Director **Cathe Jacobi** Designers **Annie Liebert, Joseph Williams** and **Jay Roger** Client **Warner Brothers Studio Store**

POWERPUFF GIRLS
saving the world before bedtime
POWERPUFF GIRLS
BB

WARNER STUDIO
BROS. STORE
CARTOON NETWORK
O STORE
WARNER BROS.

THE POWERPUFF GIRLS

(this spread) Design Firm **Sussman/Prejza & Co., Inc.** Creative and Art Director **Deborah Sussman** Designers **Jennifer Stroller, Paula Loh, Tad Hara, Paul Nagakoura** and **Fernando Vasquez** Photographer **Jim Simmons/Annette del Zoppo Prod.** Client **The Rouse Co., Columbia, MD**

Regal
Cinema
Restaurants
Bed Bath
& Beyond
Parisian
Food Court
Dillard's

2b

(this spread) Design Firm **Hornall Anderson Design Works** Art Director **Jack Anderson** Designers **Jack Anderson, Mary Hermes, Gretchen Cook, Andrew Smith, Alan Florsheim** and **Cliff Chung** Illustrators **Gretchen Cook** and **Andrew Smith** Naming Consultant **Tyler Cartier** Client **Space Needle**

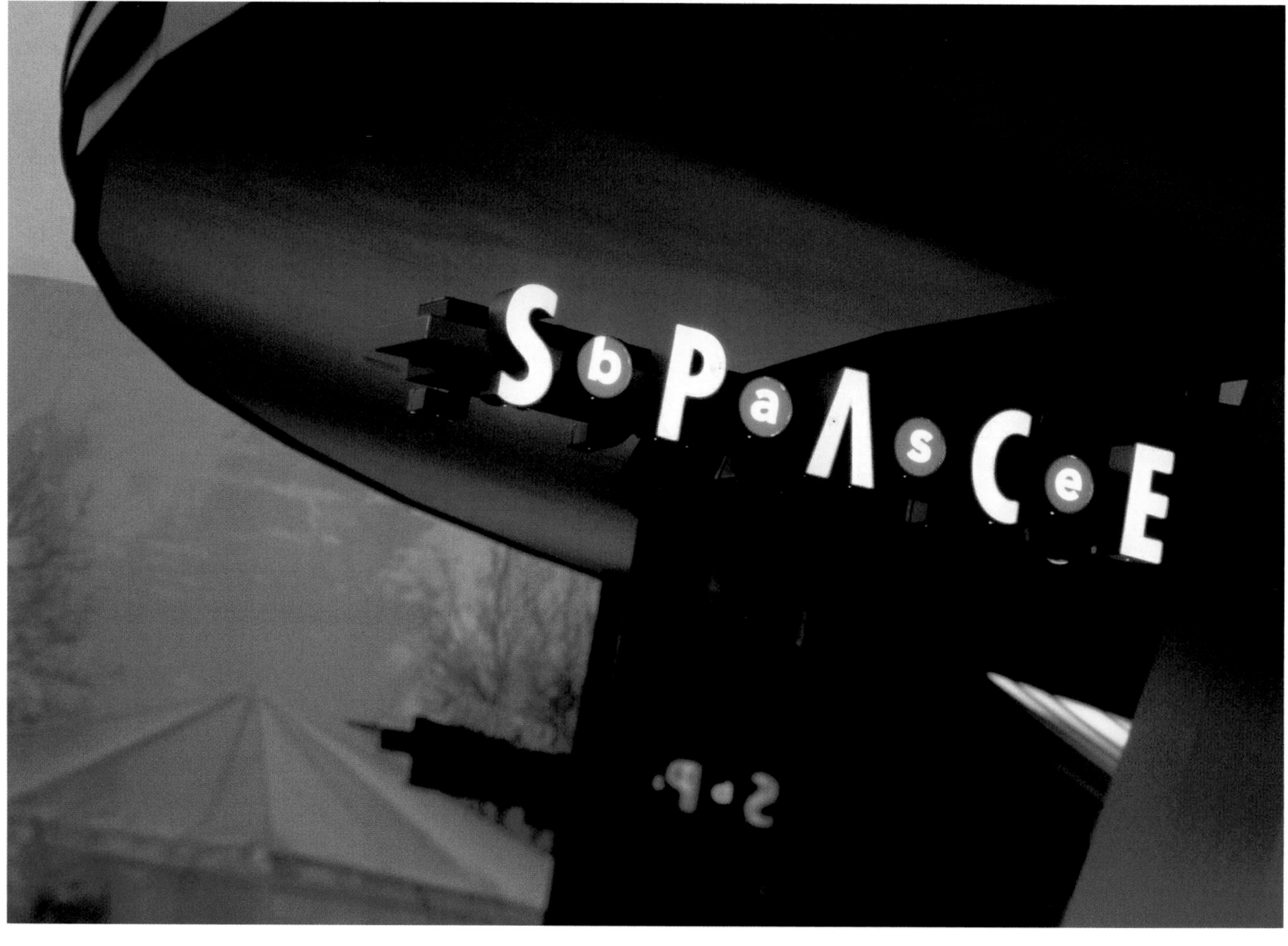

space needle
space needle

215
4th
Ave. N
Seattle

space needle
space needle

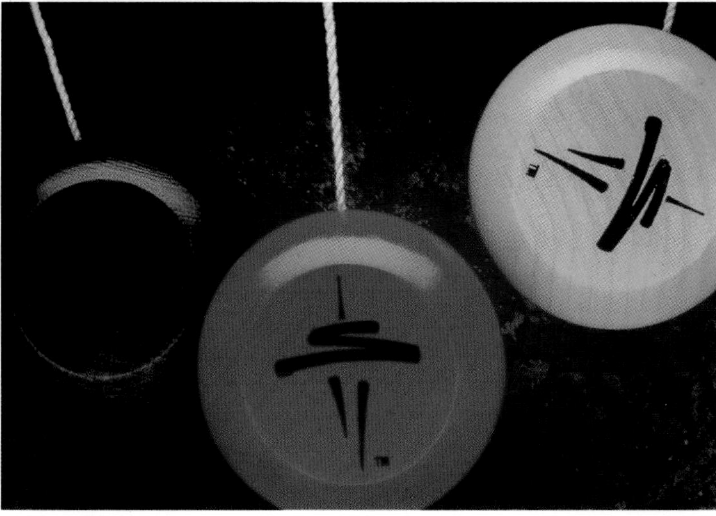

space needle
space needle
space needle

Design Firm **Lorenc & Yoo Design** Creative Director **Jan Lorenc** Art Directors **Jan Lorenc** and **Rory Myers** Designers **David Park, Gary Flesher, Steve McCall** and **Chung Youl Yoo** Photograph

Rion Rizzo Illustrators **Rory Myers** & **Matthew Porter** Client **Lifetime Television NYC** (opposite) Design Firm **Sammy** Copywriter **Beth Cochran** Client **Pennsylvania Real Estate Investment Trus**

PENNSYLVANIA REAL ESTATE INVESTMENT TRUST
PREIT-RUBIN, INC. MANAGEMENT AFFILIATE
Real Estate Investment
Trust

ner **Mark Rayner** Client **Melbourne Sports & Aquatic Centre**

(this spread) Design Firm **Pentagram Design** Art Director **Woody Pirtle** Designers **Woody Pirtle, Tracey Cameron** and **Karen Parolek** Client **Fujisankei Communications Group**

(this page, left) Design Firm **Lorenc & Yoo Design** Creative Director **Jan Lorenc** Art Directors **Jan Lorenc** and **Beth Cochran** Designers **Steve McCall, David Park, Chung Youl Yoo** and **Susie Caldwell** Photographer **Rion Rizzo** Illustrator **Susie Caldwell** Client **Zamias** (this page, right, and opposite page) Design Firm **Lorenc & Yoo Design** Creative Directors **Jan Lorenc** and **Beth Cochran** Art Director **Jan Lorenc** Designers **David Park, Veda Sammy** and **Steve McCall** Photographer **Rion Rizzo** Illustrator **Veda Sammy** Copywriter **Beth Cochran** Client **First Union Management**

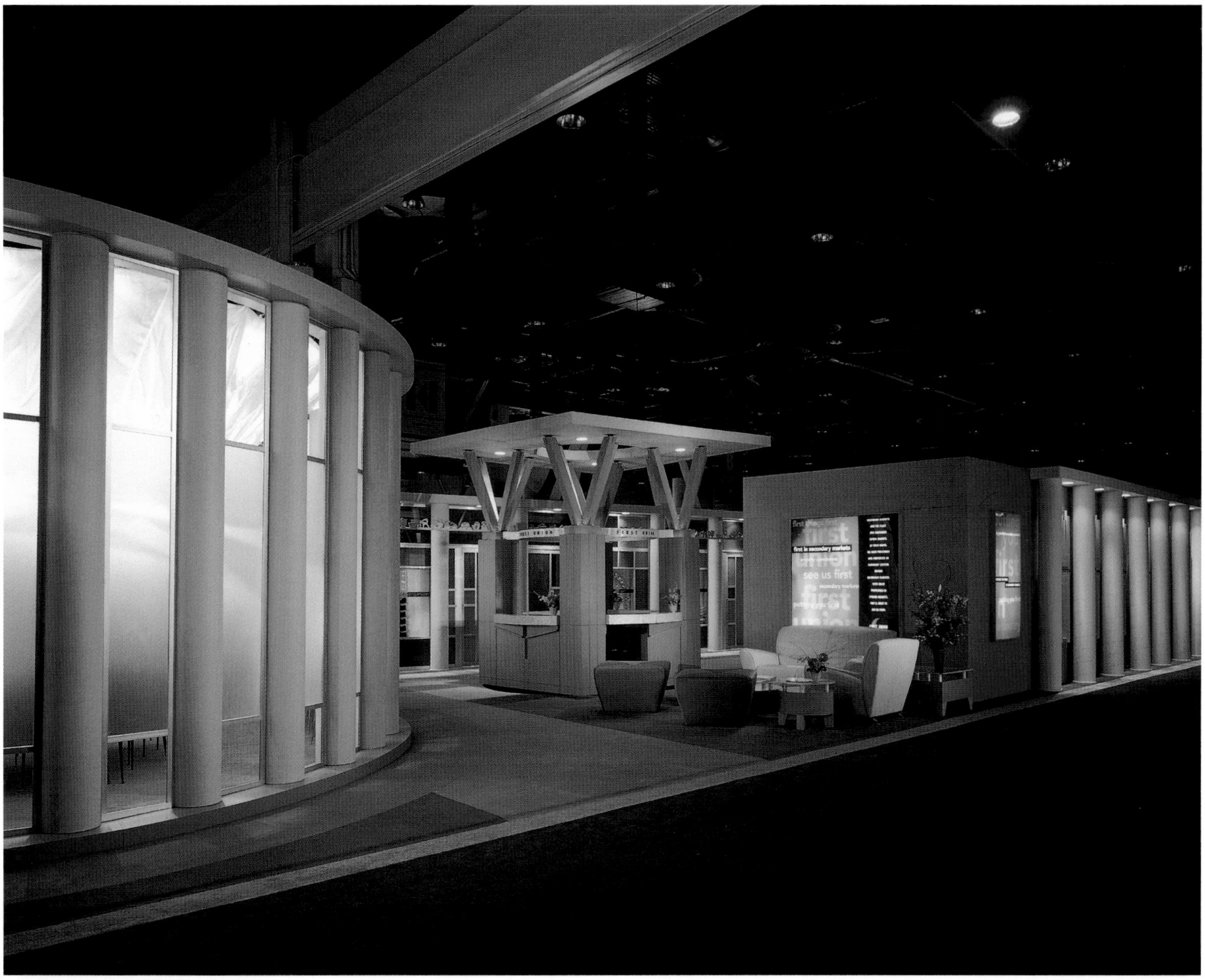

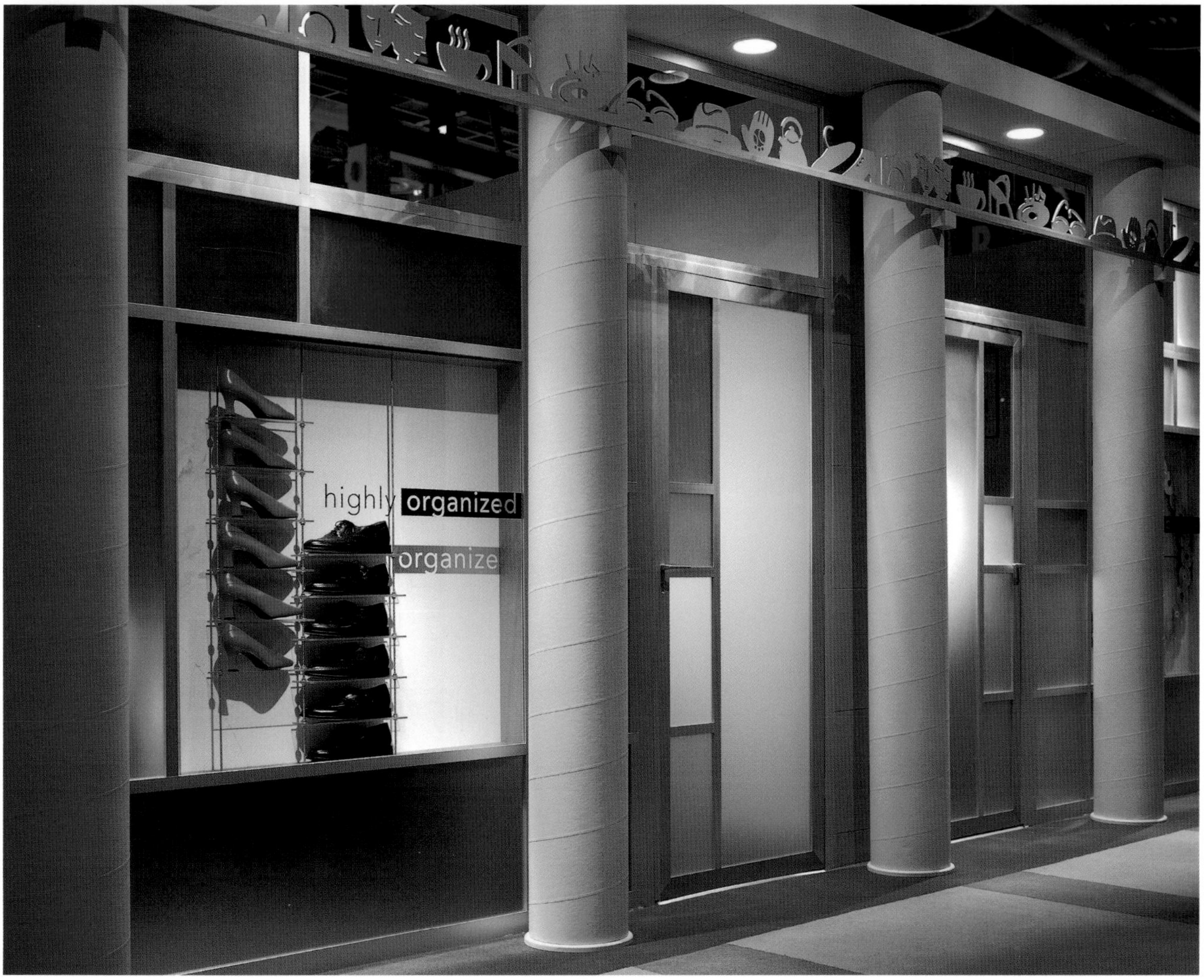
highly organized
organize

(this spread) Design Firm **Siegelgale** Creative Director **Kenneth Cooke** Art Director **Diane DePaolis** Designers **Jed Davis** and **Tina Feiertag** Photographer **Julie Powel** Client **Woodstock Film Festival**

REACHING NEW HEIGHTS OF INDEPENDENCE
SEPTEMBER 21 - 24, 2000
PO Box 1406, Woodstock, NY 12498, info@woodstockfilmfestival.com
www.woodstockfilmfestival.com
WOODSTOCK FILM FESTIVAL
SPONSORS
siegelgale

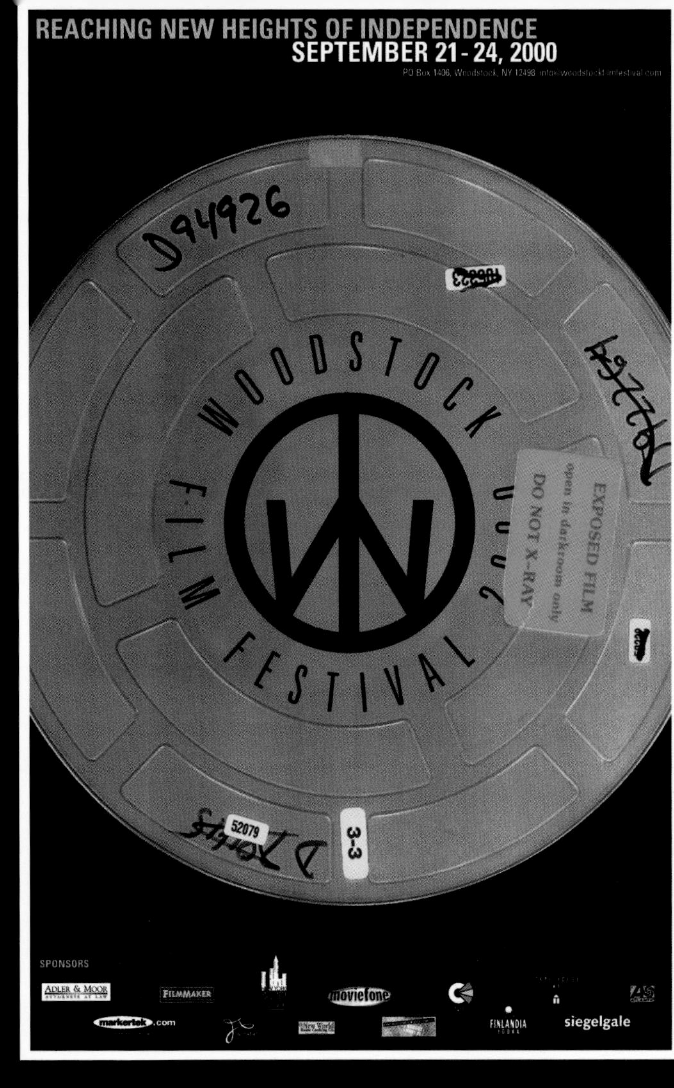
REACHING NEW HEIGHTS OF INDEPENDENCE
SEPTEMBER 21 - 24, 2000
WOODSTOCK FILM FESTIVAL 2000
EXPOSED FILM
open in darkroom only
DO NOT X-RAY
SPONSORS
siegelgale

WOODSTOCK FILM FESTIVAL 2000

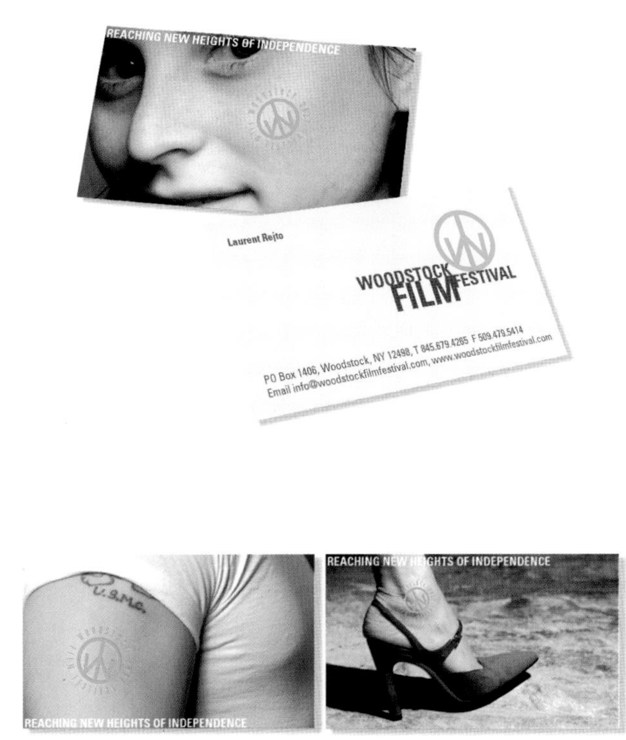
REACHING NEW HEIGHTS OF INDEPENDENCE
Laurent Rejto
WOODSTOCK FILM FESTIVAL
PO Box 1406, Woodstock, NY 12498, T 845.679.4265 F 509.479.5414
Email info@woodstockfilmfestival.com, www.woodstockfilmfestival.com
REACHING NEW HEIGHTS OF INDEPENDENCE
REACHING NEW HEIGHTS OF INDEPENDENCE

(this spread) Design Firm **Calori & Vanden-Eynden** Designers **Chris Calori, Marisa Schulman** and **Denise Funaro** Photographer **Bill Miller** Client **American Institute of Graphic Arts, New York Chapter**

AIGA/COLLISION
Registration
A-G
AIGA/COLLISION
Registration
H-O
AIGA/COLLISION
Registration
P-Z

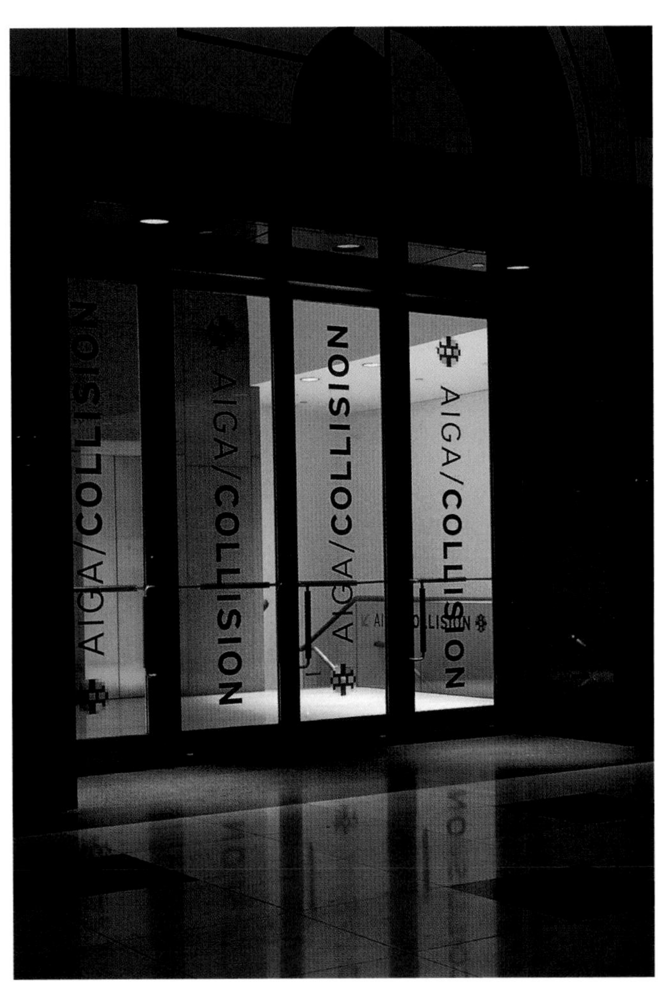
AIGA/COLLISION
AIGA/COLLISION
AIGA/COLLISION
AIGA/COLLISION

Pentagram Design Creative Director **Kit Hinrichs** Art Director **Brian Jacobs** Designers **Brian Jacobs** and **Brian Cox** Client **American Institute of Graphic Arts**

Friday, October 6
Saturday, October 7
Sunday, October 8

AIGA

Risk/Reward
Sponsors
Presenting Sponsors
Potlatch
AQUENT
Supporting Sponsor
razorfish
Student Host
Crane's
With additional support from
Critique magazine

(this and following spread) Design Firm **Lorenc & Yoo Design** Creative and Art Director **Jan Lorenc** Designers **John Laurer** and **Rory Myers** Photographer **Rion Rizzo** Architect **Gary Flesher** Client **Georgia Pacific**

G-P SALES FORCE
Independent Retailers
Multi-Location Retailers
Manufactured Housing
Industrial

19 10

Building Material Retailers
GP

(this spread) Creative and Art Director **Kit Hinrichs** Photographer **Lucca Pioltelli** Client **American Institute of Graphic Arts**

X

(this spread) Design Firm **USWeb/CKS** Creative Director **Andy Dreyfus** Designers **Eric Wendt, Tim Kobe, Mike Dolan, Wilhelm Oehl, Patti Glover, Aki Shelton, Amy Wyler** and **Dana Ahlfeldt** Client **Apple Computer**

(this and following spread) Design Firm **Hirano Studio** Creative Director **Aoshi Kudo** Art Director and Designer **Keiko Hirano** Photographer **Yasuo Saji** Copywriter **Lang Phipps** Client **Shiseido Co., Ltd.**

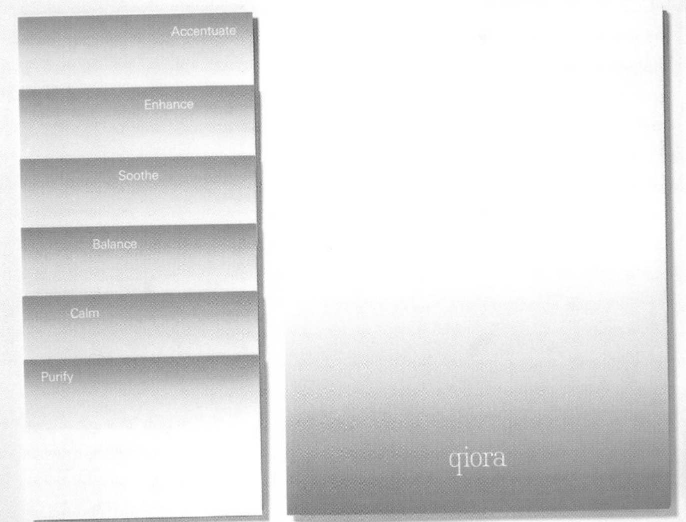
Accentuate
Enhance
Soothe
Balance
Calm
Purify
qiora

qiora

qiora
qiora
qiora
qiora

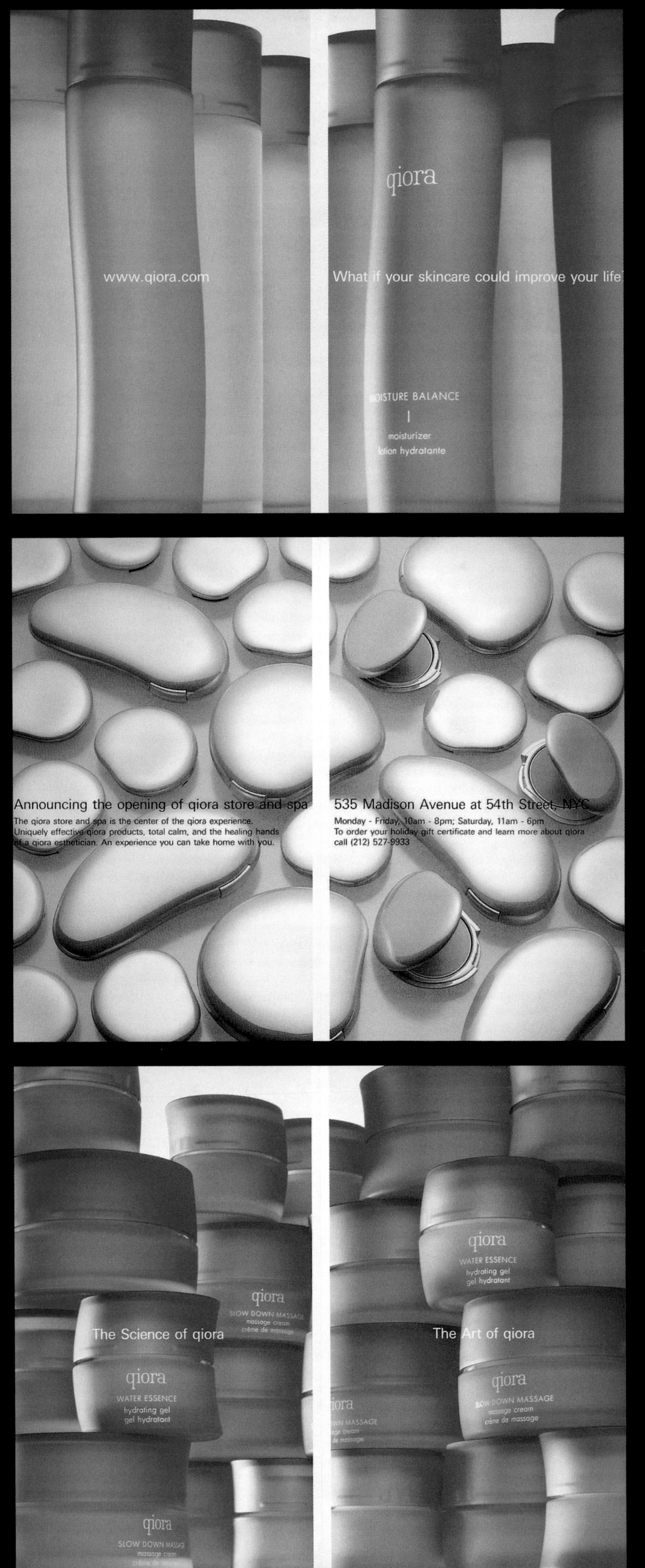
qiora
www.qiora.com
What if your skincare could improve your life?
MOISTURE BALANCE
I
moisturizer
lotion hydratante
Announcing the opening of qiora store and spa
The qiora store and spa is the center of the qiora experience.
Uniquely effective qiora products, total calm, and the healing hands
of a qiora esthetician. An experience you can take home with you.
535 Madison Avenue at 54th Street, NYC
Monday - Friday, 10am - 8pm; Saturday, 11am - 6pm
To order your holiday gift certificate and learn more about qiora
call (212) 527-9933
The Science of qiora
The Art of qiora
qiora
WATER ESSENCE
hydrating gel
gel hydratant
qiora
SLOW DOWN MASSAGE
massage cream
crème de massage

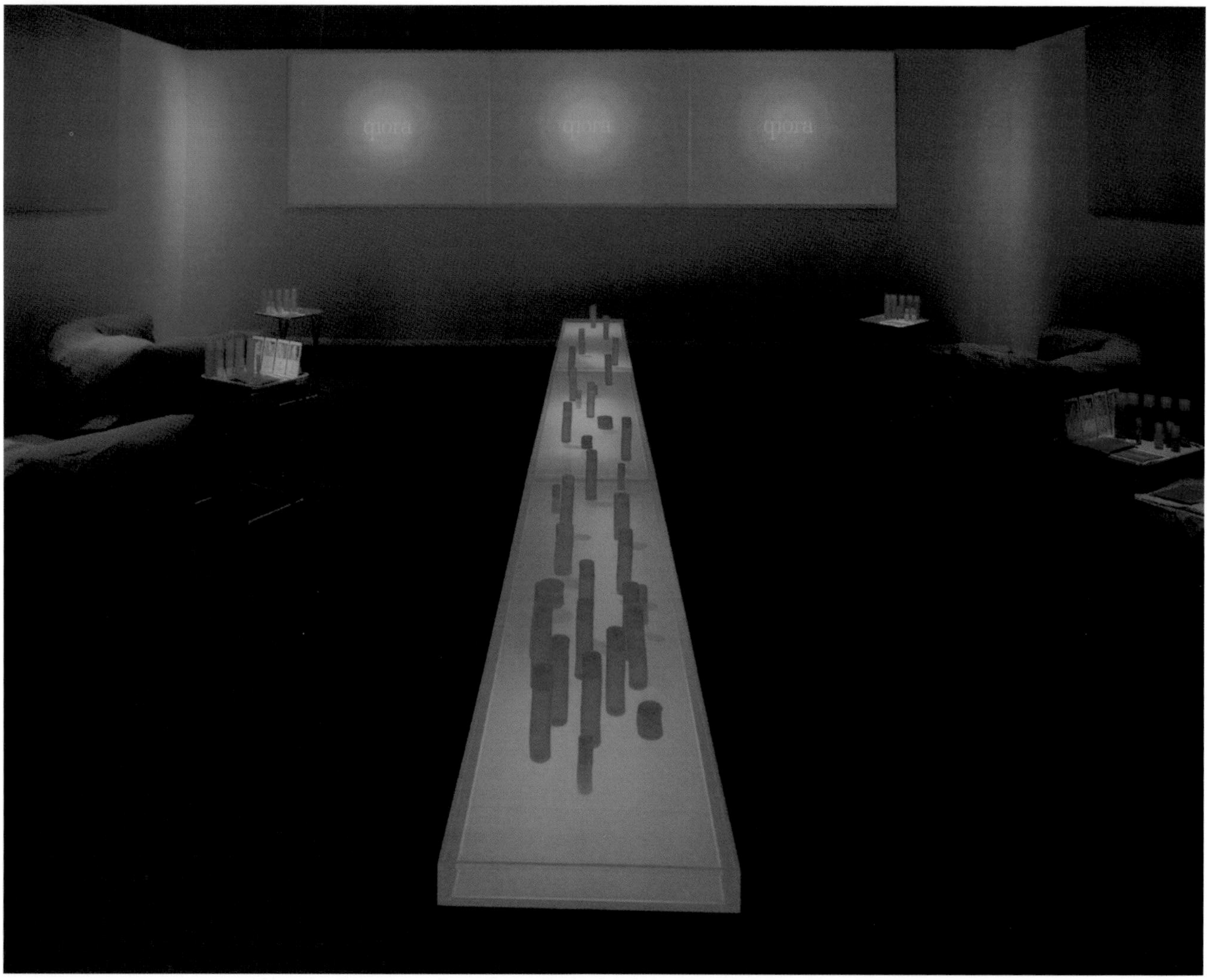

(this spread) Design Firm **Shiseido Creation DVS** Creative Director **Shyuichi Ikeda** Art Director **Aoshi Kudo** Designers **Aoshi Kudo** and **Rikiya Vekusa** Film Director **Hiroyuki Nakano** Lighting Designer **Harumi Fujimoto** Client **Shiseido Co., Ltd.**

m **Pentagram Design** Designers **Michael Bierut** and **Esther Bridavsky** Architects **James Biber** and **Michael Zweck-Bronner** Photographer **James Shanks** Client **Fashion Center**

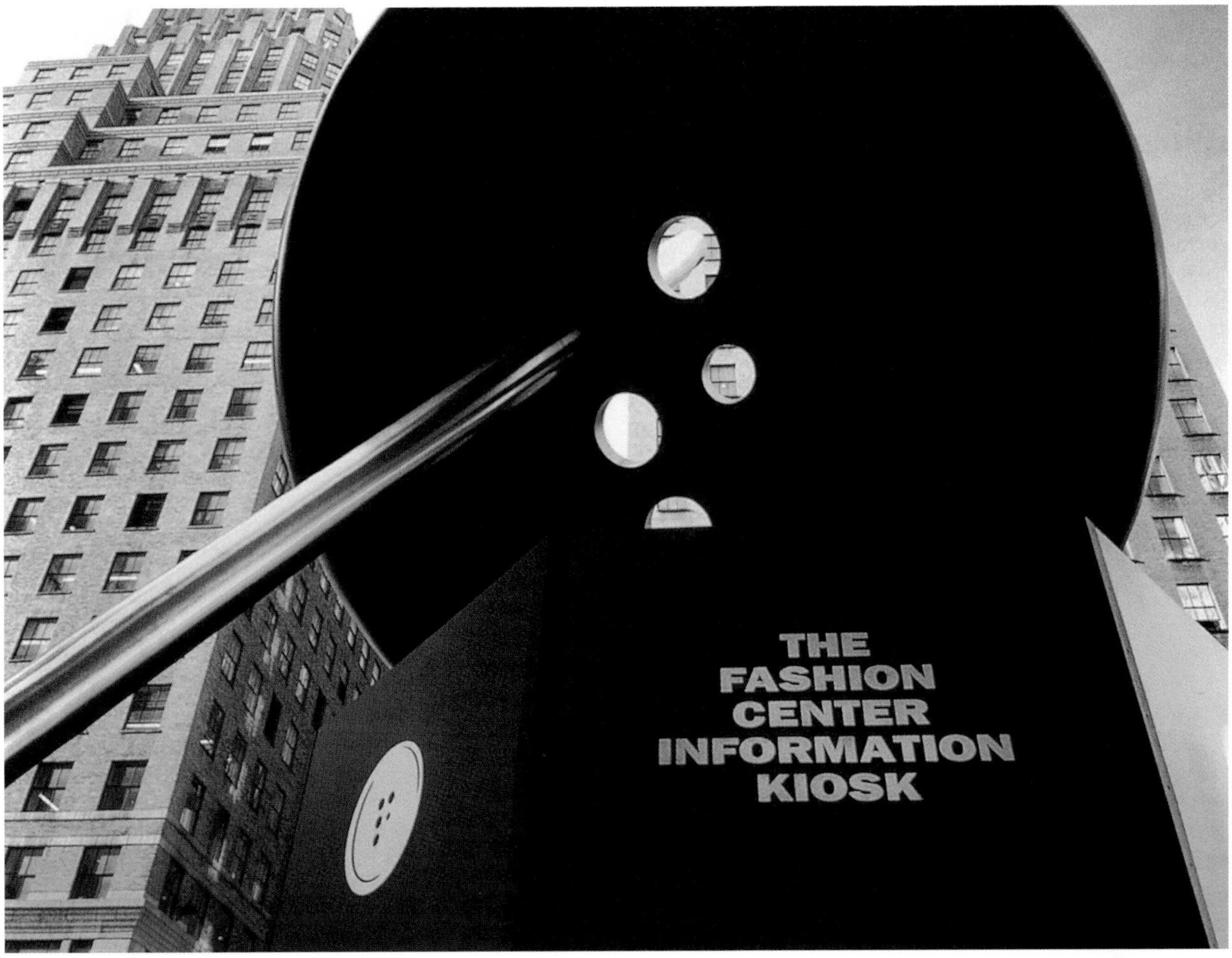

(this spread) Design Firm **Pentagram Design** Designers **Paula Scher** and **Anke Stohlmann** Client **Anne Klein**

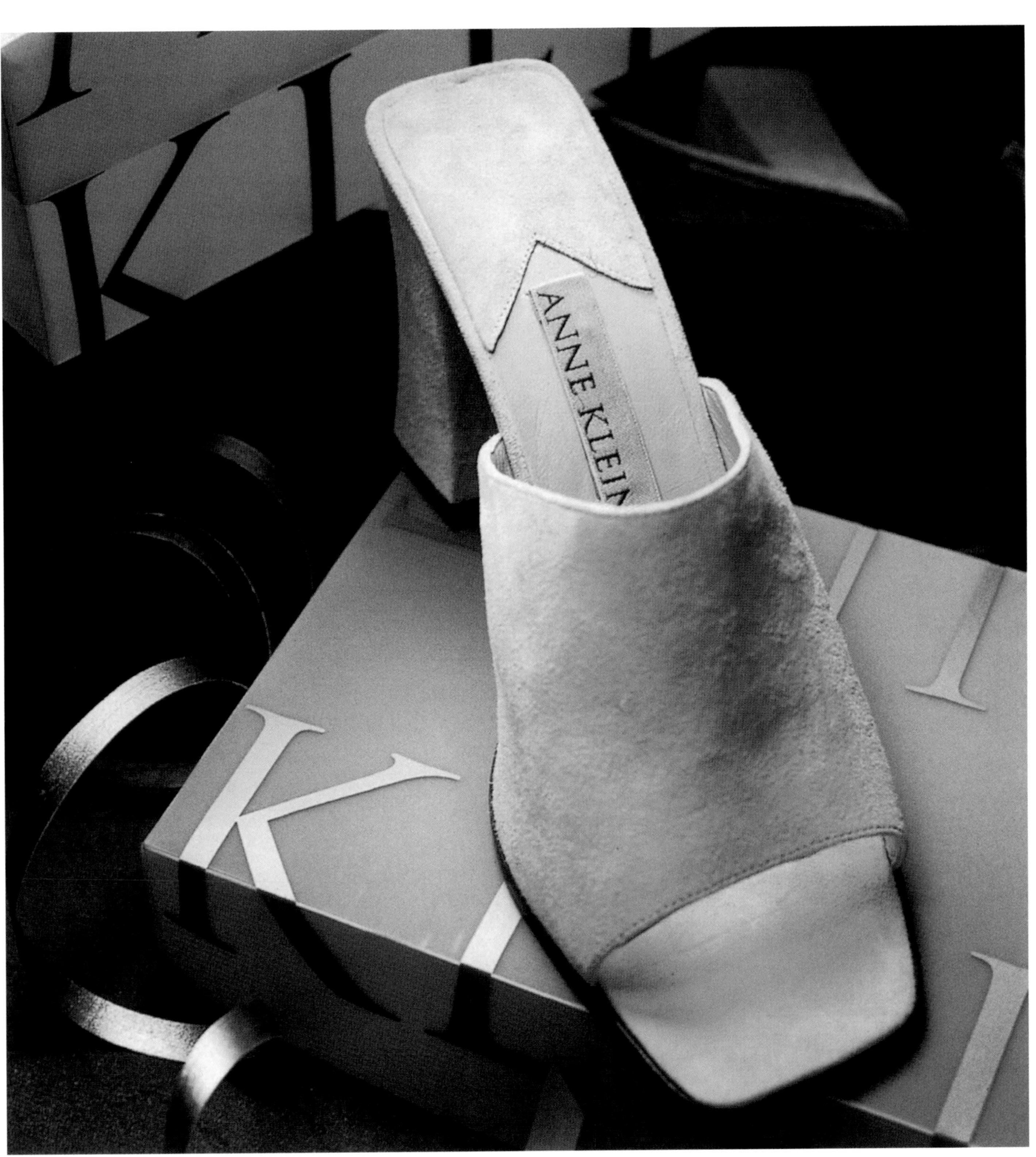
ANNE KLEI

(this spread) Design Firm **Turner Duckworth** Creative Directors **David Turner** and **Bruce Duckworth** Designer **David Turner** Photographer **Michael Lamotte** Client **Golden State International**

OLOGI
FLEX | OLOGI

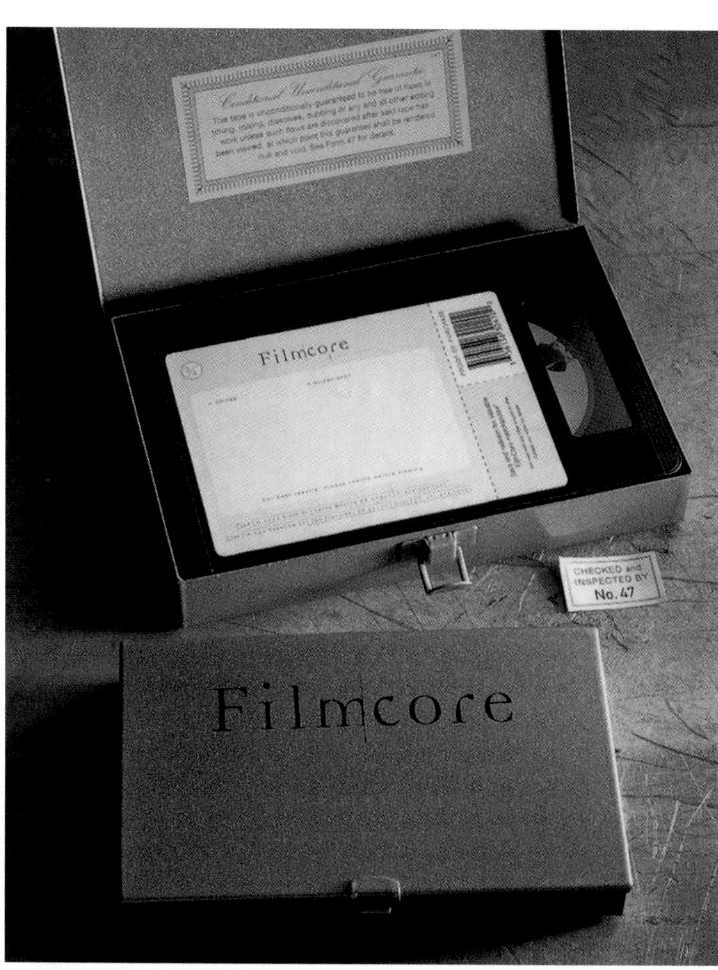

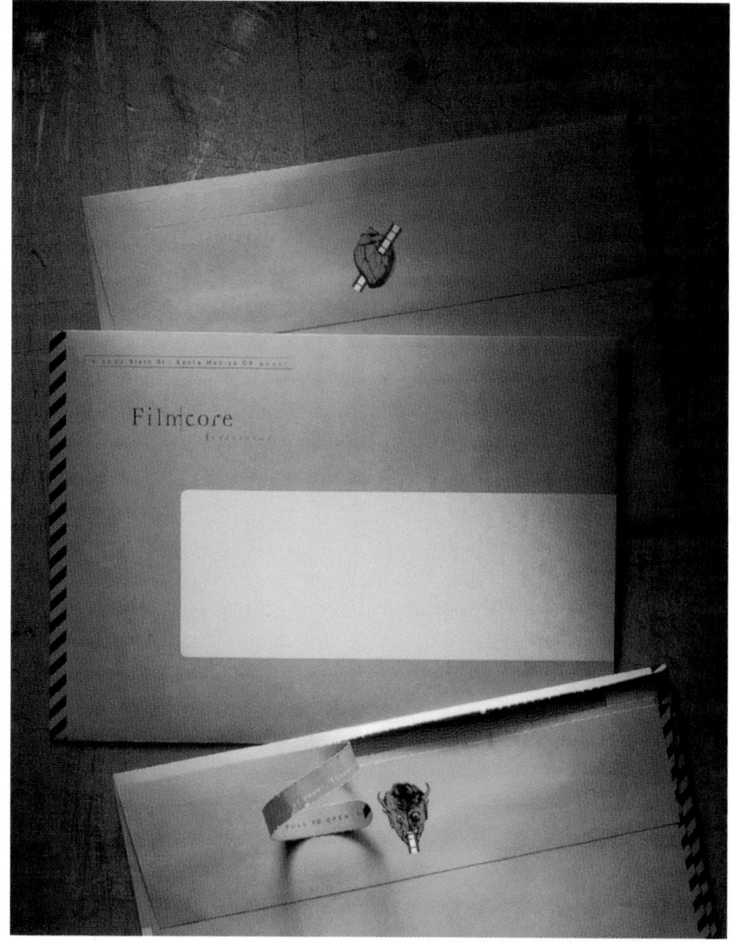

(this spread) Design Firm **Sandstrom Design** Creative and Art Director **Steve Sandstrom** Copywriter **Steve Sandoz** Client **Filmcore**

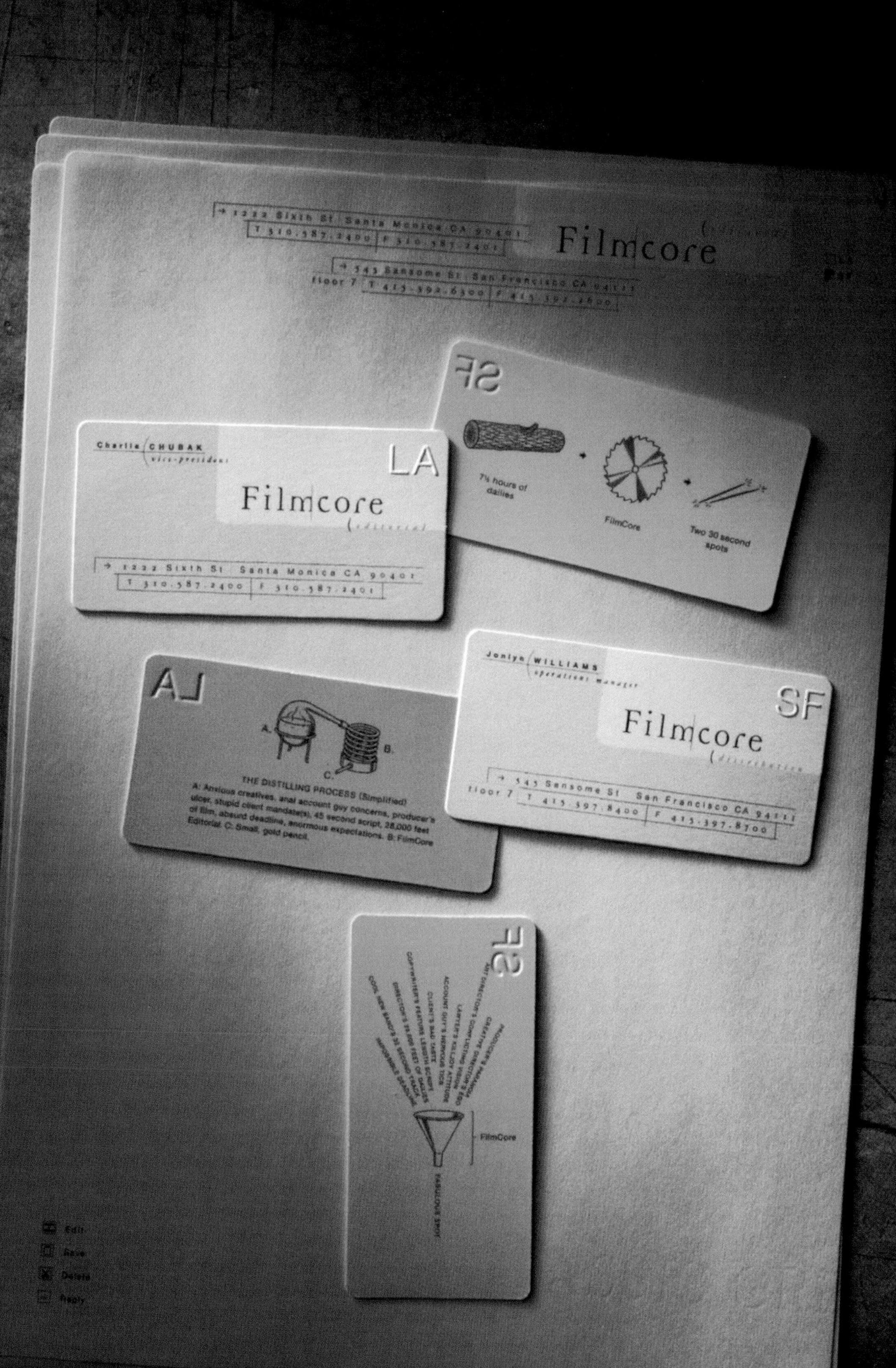
→ 1222 Sixth St Santa Monica CA 90401
T 310.587.2400 F 310.587.2401
Filmcore
→ 545 Sansome St San Francisco CA 94111
floor 7
Charlie CHUBAK
vice-president
LA
Filmcore
(editorial)
→ 1222 Sixth St Santa Monica CA 90401
T 310.587.2400 F 310.587.2401
SF
7½ hours of dailies
FilmCore
Two 30 second spots
LA
A.
B.
C.
THE DISTILLING PROCESS (Simplified)
A: Anxious creatives, anal account guy concerns, producer's ulcer, stupid client mandate(s), 45 second script, 28,000 feet of film, absurd deadline, enormous expectations. B: FilmCore Editorial. C: Small, gold pencil.
Jonlyn WILLIAMS
operations manager
SF
Filmcore
(distribution)
→ 545 Sansome St San Francisco CA 94111
floor 7 T 415.397.8400 F 415.397.8700
SF
FilmCore
FABULOUS SPOT
Edit
Save
Delete
Reply

Design Art Director **José A. Serrano** Designer **Jeff Samaripa** Photographer **David Deahl** Illustrator **Miguel Perez** Client **Big Deahl Inc.**

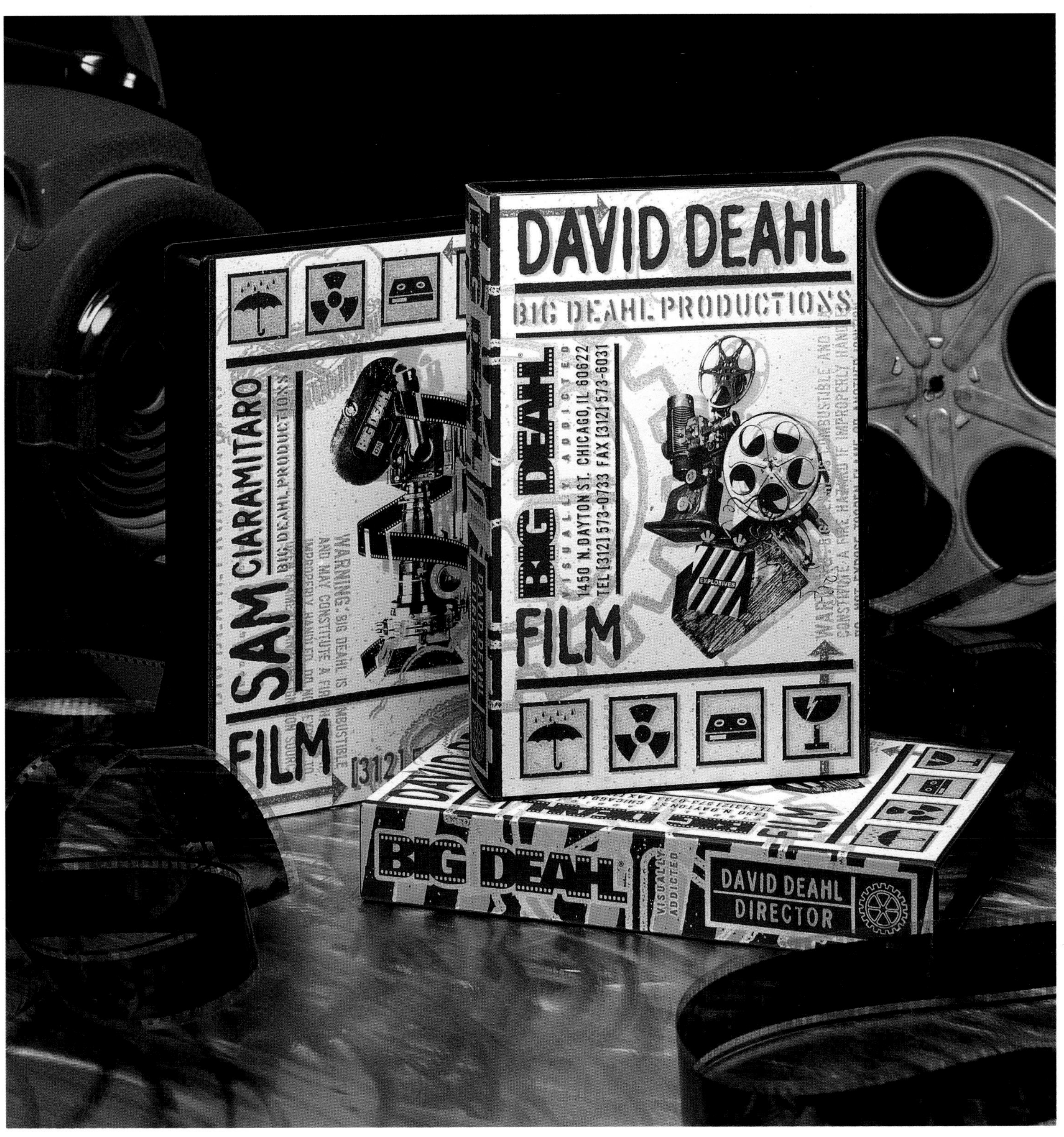
DAVID DEAHL
BIG DEAHL PRODUCTIONS
BIG DEAHL
VISUALLY ADDICTED
1450 N.DAYTON ST. CHICAGO, IL 60622
TEL [312] 573-0733 FAX [312] 573-6031
FILM
EXPLOSIVES
DAVID DEAHL DIRECTOR
SAM CIARAMITARO
BIG DEAHL PRODUCTIONS
FILM
BIG DEAHL
VISUALLY ADDICTED
DAVID DEAHL
DIRECTOR

(this and following spread) Design Firm **Summa** Creative Director **Josep Maria Mir** Art Director **Wladimir Marnich** Designers **Anna Sodupe** and **Wladimir Marnich** Illustrator **Anna Sodupe** Client **Miquel Alimentacio**

SUMA
SUMA
SUMA

SUMA
SP
B-0928-NK

SUMA
SUMA

POPS
SARDINES
PALAIA
BRUIXA
ESCOPINYA
CLÒISSES
LLAMÀNTOL
OSTRES
CALAMARSET
LLUÇ
GALL
SUMA
MANDONGUILLA
BISTEC
MANXEGO
ROSBIF
FORMATGE
VEDELLA
MORTADEL·LA
PORC
GUATLLES
CRANC
ESCAMARLANS
GAMBA
VERAT
XAI
EMMENTAL

BAGUETTE
COCA
SUMA
MAGDALENES
PA
MAGDALENA
FLECA
SECALL
BRIOIX
XURRO
GALETA
FORN
CROISSANT
ENSAÏMADES
PANELLET
CANYA
PANETS
CROISSANTS
BARRA
ULLERES
PASTÍS
BASTONET
PANET
BUNYOLS

(this spread) Design Firm **Hornall Anderson Design Works** Art Directors **Jack Anderson** and **Larry Anderson** Designers **Jack Anderson, Larry Anderson, Bruce Stigler, Ed Lee, Bruce Branson-Meyer, Michael Brugman, Mary Chin Hutchinson** and **Kaye Farmer** Copywriter **Pamela Mason Davey** Client **Widmer Brothers**

HOP JACK
WIDMER BROTHERS
pale ale

HEFEWEIZEN
wheat beer
HOP JACK
pale ale
SPRINGFEST
alt beer
WIDMER BROTHERS

SWEET BETTY
BUCKET O' BETTY'S

SPRINGFEST
alt beer
Springfest: Quenches
HEFEWEIZEN
wheat beer
"America's Original Hefeweizen."
WIDBERRY
"Widmer Brothers Widberry"

SWEET BETTY
HEFEWEIZEN
WIDBERRY
HOP JACK
WIDMER BROTHERS

(this spread) Design Firm **Karacters Design Group** Creative Director **Maria Kennedy** Art Directors **Matthew Clark** and **Roy White** Designer **Matthew Clark** Photographer **Raeff Miles** Client **Overwaitea Food Group**

Mushroom and
Gorgonzola Tondi
1.99
100 g
Mushroom and egg
striped pasta filled
with mushrooms and
gorgonzola cheese

URBAN
FARE
URBAN
FARE
URBAN
FARE
$7.50

LEAVE
THE GUN.
TAKE
THE
CANNOLIS.

(this spread) Design Firm **The Way Group** Creative Director **Nin Glaister** Designer **Kristina de Corpo** Lettering **Andy Benedek** Client **Balducci's**

Balducci's
GUARANTEED FINEST QUALITY BY BALDUCCI'S
BUON APPETITO!
SINCE 1916
Balducci's
EST 1916
Balducci's
FIG JAM
Balducci's
PEACH JAM

(this spread) Design Firm **CLM Design** Creative and Art Director **Gail Letcher** Designers **Gail Letcher** and **John Bulter** Photographer **Jeffery Dow** Client **Swopper**

movement architecture · sitting in motion
swo)pper

swo)pper
P O Box 19068, Reno, Nevada 89511 · toll free: 1-866-SWOPPER · (V) 775.851.7967 · (F) 775.851.7969 · www.swopperusa.com
a division of aeris USA

(this spread) Design Firm **Coande Network for Communication and Design** Creative Directors **Katharina Leuenberger** and **Peter Vetter** Designer **Mischa Leiner** Strategy Consulting **Dr. Thomas Bernold** Client **Liechtensteinische Post AG, Vaduz (Liechtenstein)**
Notes: The project represents the proposal for a new conception of naming, branding and design system for the new corporation of the post services of the country of Liechtenstein. The project has not been realized.

FLex
3,40

FLex
3,40

FLex
3,40

FLex
3,40

(this spread) Design Firm **Scandinavian Design Group** Creative Director **Gary Swindell** Art Director **Bard Annweiler** Designers **Morten Fornebo** and **Knut Bang** Photographer **Jarle Nyttingnes** Client **Aetat**

jobb til mennesker, mennesker til jobben

aetat

aetat
informasjon

(this spread) Design Firm **Coande Network for Communication and Design** in collaboration with **Vignelli Associates, New York** Creative Directors **Katharina Leuenberger** and **Peter Vetter** Designers **Mischa Leiner, Yuji Yamazaki** and **Dani Piedermann** Client **NASA, Public Affairs, Washington DC** Notes: It was the intention of NASA to create a new brand for the ISS (International Space Station) witch is a partnership of 14 different countries. The project has not jet been implemented.

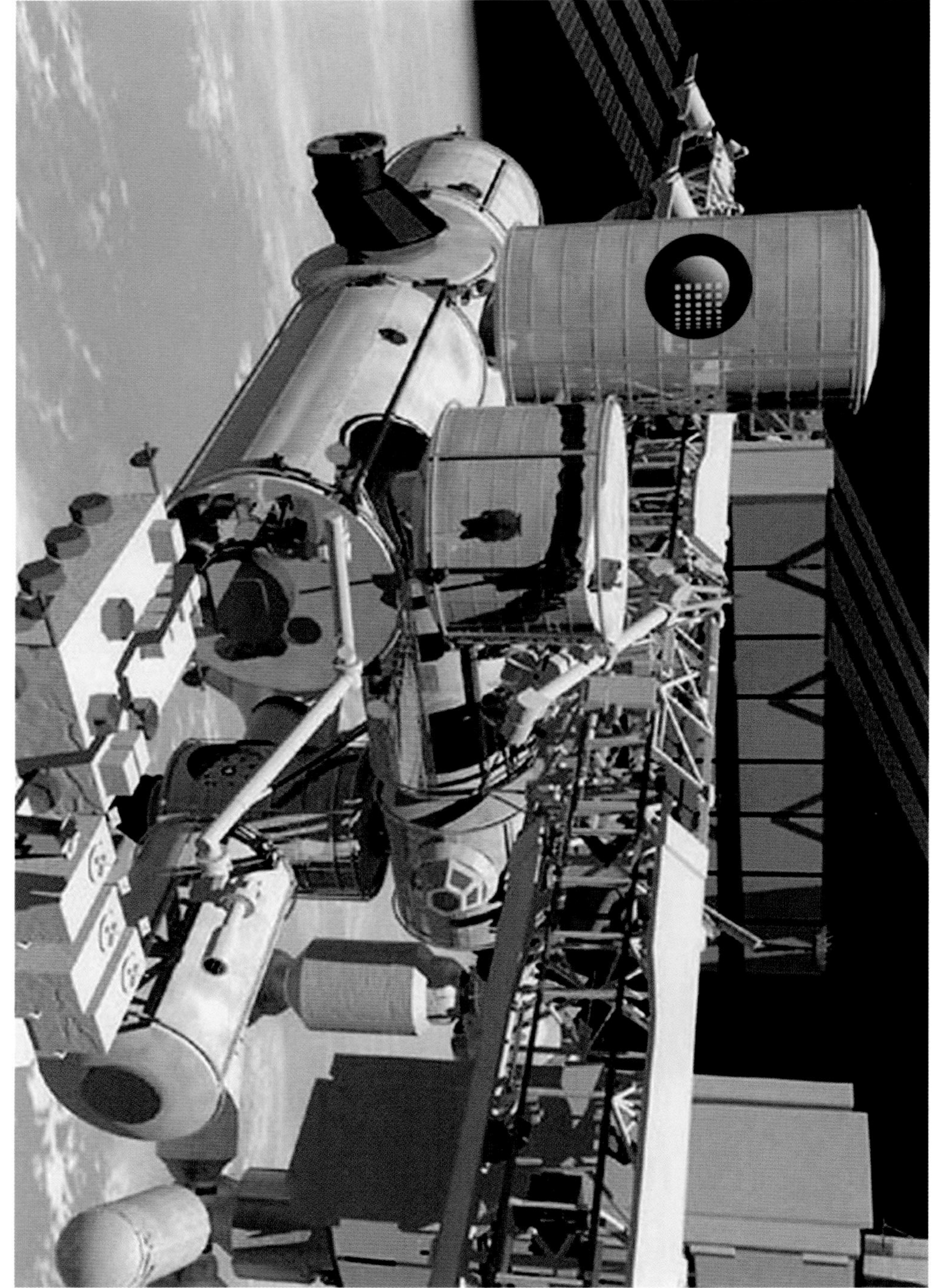

Station Spatiale Internationale
Internationale Raum-Station
International Space Station
Stazione Spaziale Internazionale
Международная Космическая Станция
国際宇宙ステーション
Estación Espacial Internacional

Communications Art Director **Louis Gagnon** Designers **Louis Gagnon** and **Francis Turgeon** Client **Developpment Germain-Des-Pres**

LE GERMAIN

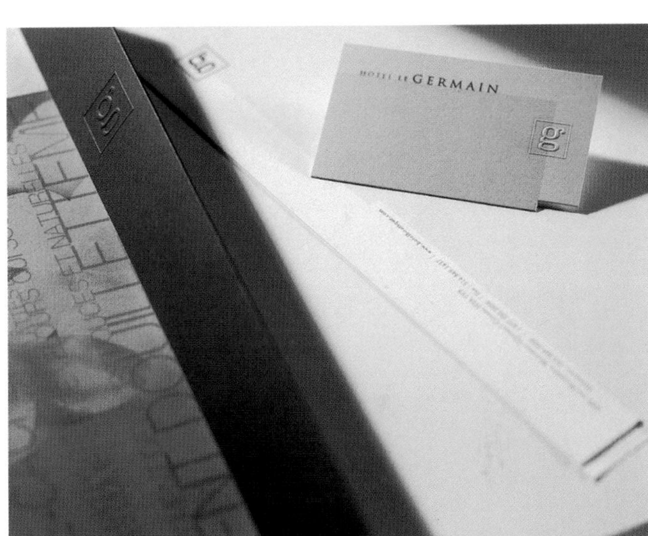
HOTEL LE GERMAIN

HOTEL LE GERMAIN
GERMAIN

HOTEL LE GERMAIN

spread) Design Firm **Templin Brink Design** Creative Director **Gaby Brink** Designer **Kris Delaney** Illustrator **Richard Borge** Copywriter **Lessley Berry** Client **Quiver Inc.**

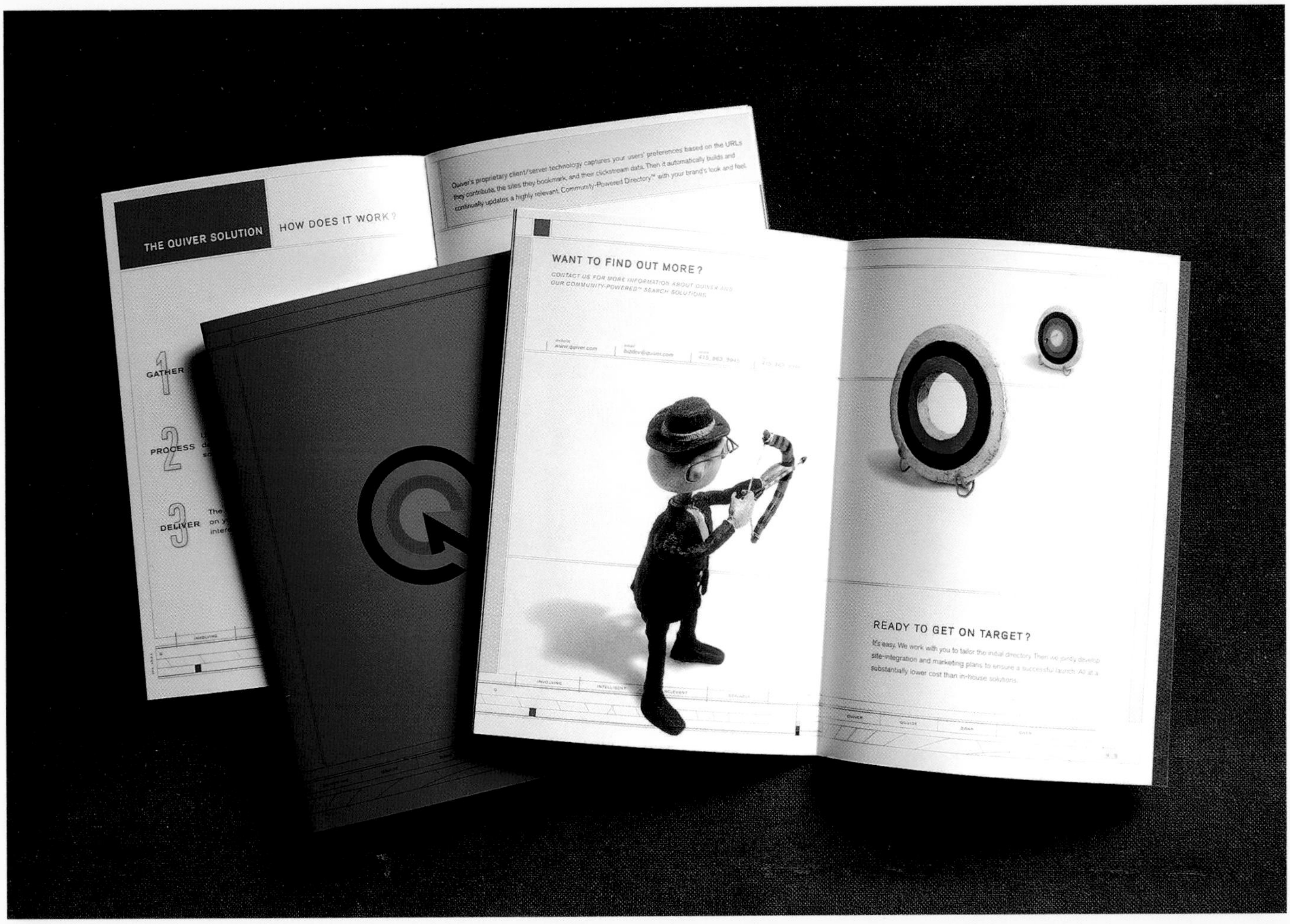
THE QUIVER SOLUTION
HOW DOES IT WORK?
GATHER
PROCESS
DELIVER
WANT TO FIND OUT MORE?
READY TO GET ON TARGET?

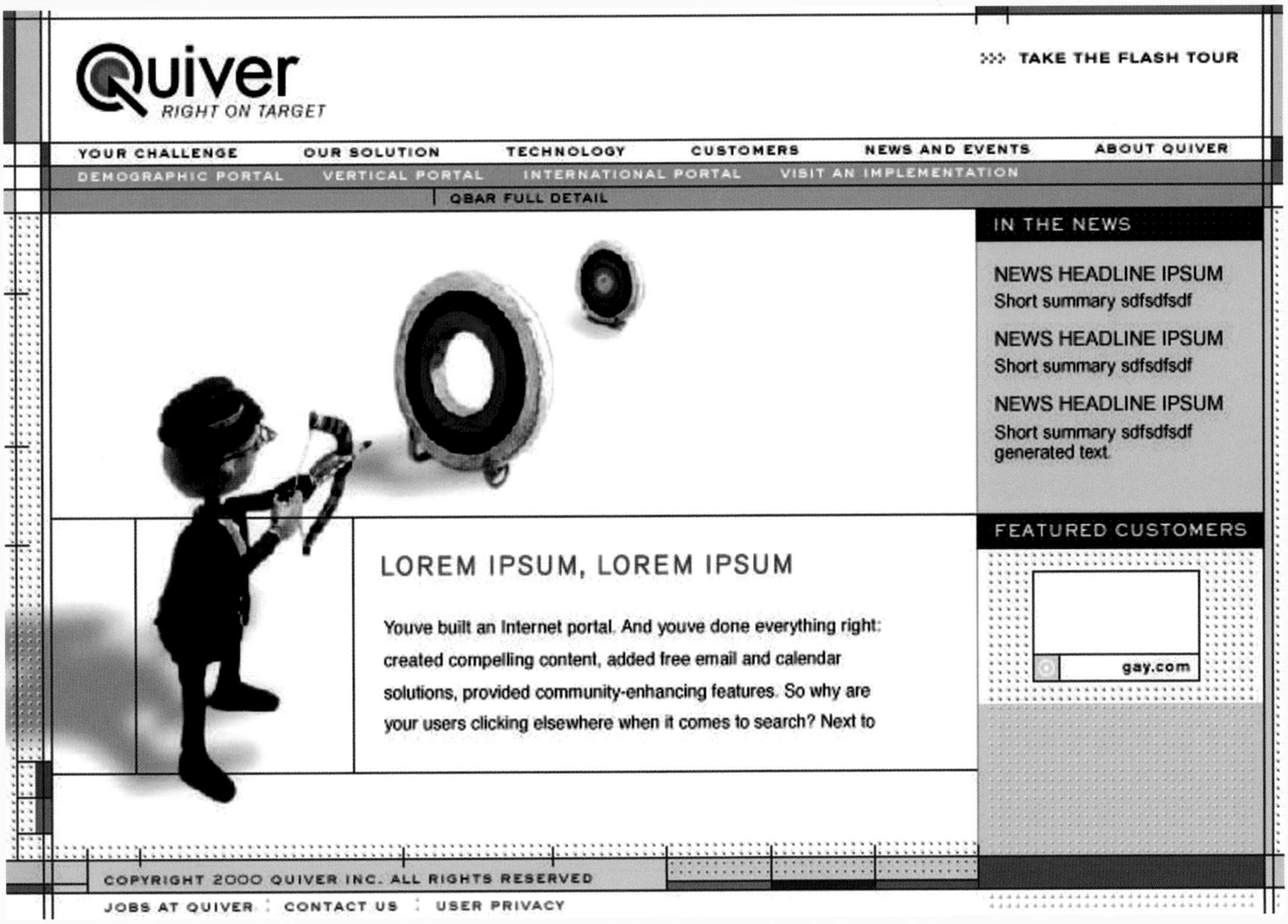
Quiver
RIGHT ON TARGET
TAKE THE FLASH TOUR
YOUR CHALLENGE
OUR SOLUTION
TECHNOLOGY
CUSTOMERS
NEWS AND EVENTS
ABOUT QUIVER
DEMOGRAPHIC PORTAL
VERTICAL PORTAL
INTERNATIONAL PORTAL
VISIT AN IMPLEMENTATION
QBAR FULL DETAIL
IN THE NEWS
NEWS HEADLINE IPSUM
Short summary sdfsdfsdf
NEWS HEADLINE IPSUM
Short summary sdfsdfsdf
NEWS HEADLINE IPSUM
Short summary sdfsdfsdf generated text.
LOREM IPSUM, LOREM IPSUM
Youve built an Internet portal. And youve done everything right: created compelling content, added free email and calendar solutions, provided community-enhancing features. So why are your users clicking elsewhere when it comes to search? Next to
FEATURED CUSTOMERS
gay.com
COPYRIGHT 2000 QUIVER INC. ALL RIGHTS RESERVED
JOBS AT QUIVER
CONTACT US
USER PRIVACY

spread) Design Firm **Hornall Anderson Design Works** Art Director **Jack Anderson** Designers **Jack Anderson, Lisa Cerveny, Mary Chin Hutchison** and **Don Stayner** Web Site Designers **Chris Sallquist, Hillary Radbill, Elmer de la Cruz, Holly Craven, Don Kenoyer, Neal McKinney, Denise Bouvet, Bryan Ebzery** and **Alan Draper** Copywriters **Pamela Mason Davey** and **Amy Bosch** Client **Twelve Horses**

Twelve Horses - Microsoft Internet Explorer
File Edit View Favorites Tools Help
Back Search Favorites History
Address http://www.12horses.com/
site map • contact • home
TWELVE HORSES
in action
partners
{power}
company
services
Welcome to Twelve Horses, the first business-to-business service company to combine the speed of electronic messaging with the power of traditional
Control Your Message
print services and literature management. We help organizations communicate efficiently, increase revenues and reduce costs quickly and easily.
Featured Areas
How our service works.
The story behind our name.
Twelve Horses seeks partnerships with strategic print and digital service companies.
Exciting career opportunities at Twelve Horses.
Done
Internet
http://www.12horses.com/company/company.html?show=legend# - Microsoft Internet Explorer
http://www.12horses.com/company/legendrevised18.swf - Microsoft Internet Explorer
{company}
imagination
power
courage
speed
Start
Inbox - Microsoft Outl...
\\Darkside\force\Clie...
http://www.12horses.c...
5:09 PM
Twelve Horses - Microsoft Internet Explorer
Address http://www.12horses.com/services/services.html
company
in action
partners
{services}
who benefits
about
how it works
FAQs
ROI calculator
pricing
contact sales
MessageMaker is a literature management and deployment tool. In its simplest terms, Messagemaker enables users to identify essential literature, create an electronic "Virtual Literature Rack®" to house this content in digital format, and then access these digital files to communicate with key audiences either electronically or via traditional print, or both. Twelve Horses hosts
how it works
description
process
difference

(this and following spread) Agency **VSA Partners, Inc.** Creative Director **James Koval** Design Director **Dan Knuckey** Designers **Rachel Middleton, Nichole Dillon, Andrew Reeves, Marcus Wiedenhoeft** and **Ashley Wasem** Photographers **Sian Kennedy** and **Chris Buck** Copywriter **Andy Blankenburg** Client **marchFIRST**

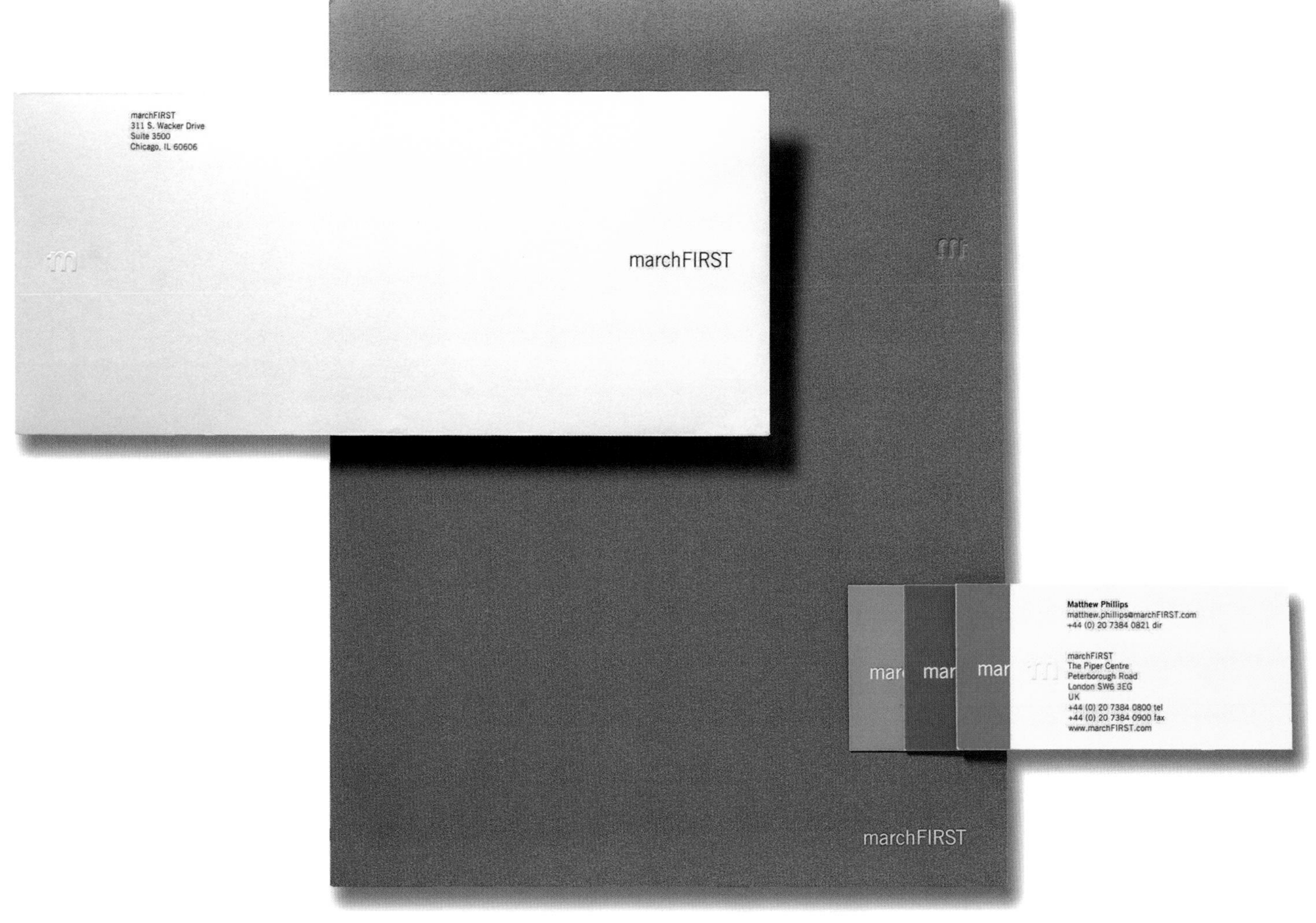

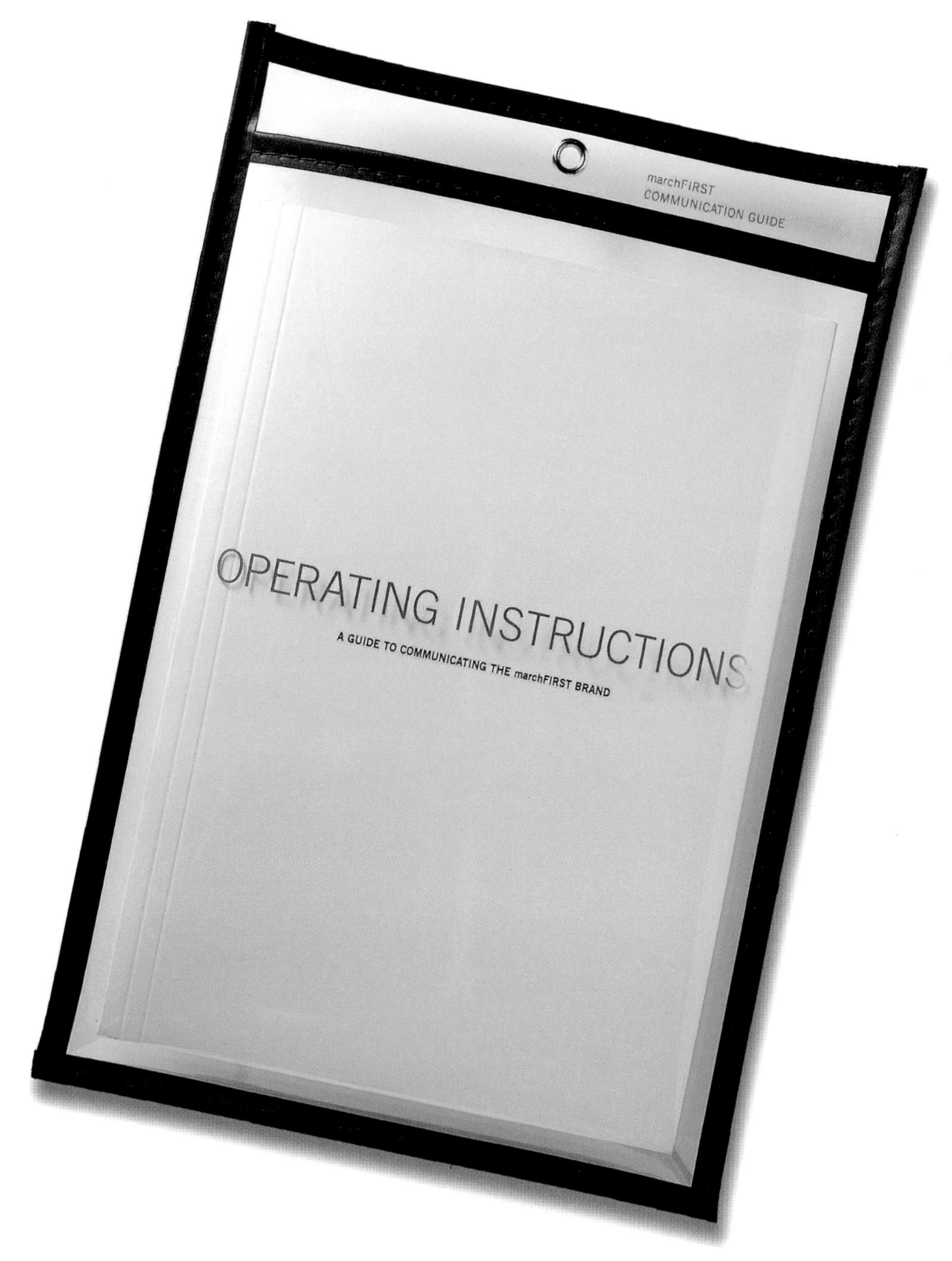
marchFIRST
COMMUNICATION GUIDE
OPERATING INSTRUCTIONS
A GUIDE TO COMMUNICATING THE marchFIRST BRAND

Michael J. Berent
michael.berent@marchfirst.com
320 N. Elizabeth Street
Chicago, IL 60607
312 913 3377 tel
312 913 6967 fax
www.marchfirst.com

marchFIRST EXISTS BECAUSE IT'S TIME FOR A NEW MODEL OF INTERNET SERVICE COMPANY.

We create winners in the digital economy by integrating, with revolutionary breadth, all of a business' stages and parts—from the inspiration behind the plan to the implementation of customized technology to the creation of a unique customer experience.

Nobody Will Build It Faster Than Us!!
m m m m
m m

"A LOGO DERIVES ITS MEANING FROM THE QUALITY OF THE THING IT SYMBOLIZES, NOT THE OTHER WAY AROUND." —Paul Rand

The marchFIRST logo is the signature of our company. It identifies us, distinguishes us and brands us. The logo is part of a visual identity system that was crafted to reflect the nature and virtues of our organization. marchFIRST is about simplicity, integration, transformation and movement, and the logo was designed with all of those messages in mind. Logos themselves do not "sell," they create connections and make impressions. The true meaning of the marchFIRST logo will be defined by the quality of our work over time and the value of our brand among our audiences. In other words, it's up to us to define the meaning of the logo through our achievements.

(this and following spread) Design Firm **Design Hoch Drei** Creative and Art Directors **Susanne Wacker, Sabine Arenz** and **Wolfram Schäffer** Designers **Sabine Arenz, Diethard Keppler** and **Nathalie Baumann** Photographer **Valentin Wormbs** Client **MAHLE GmbH**

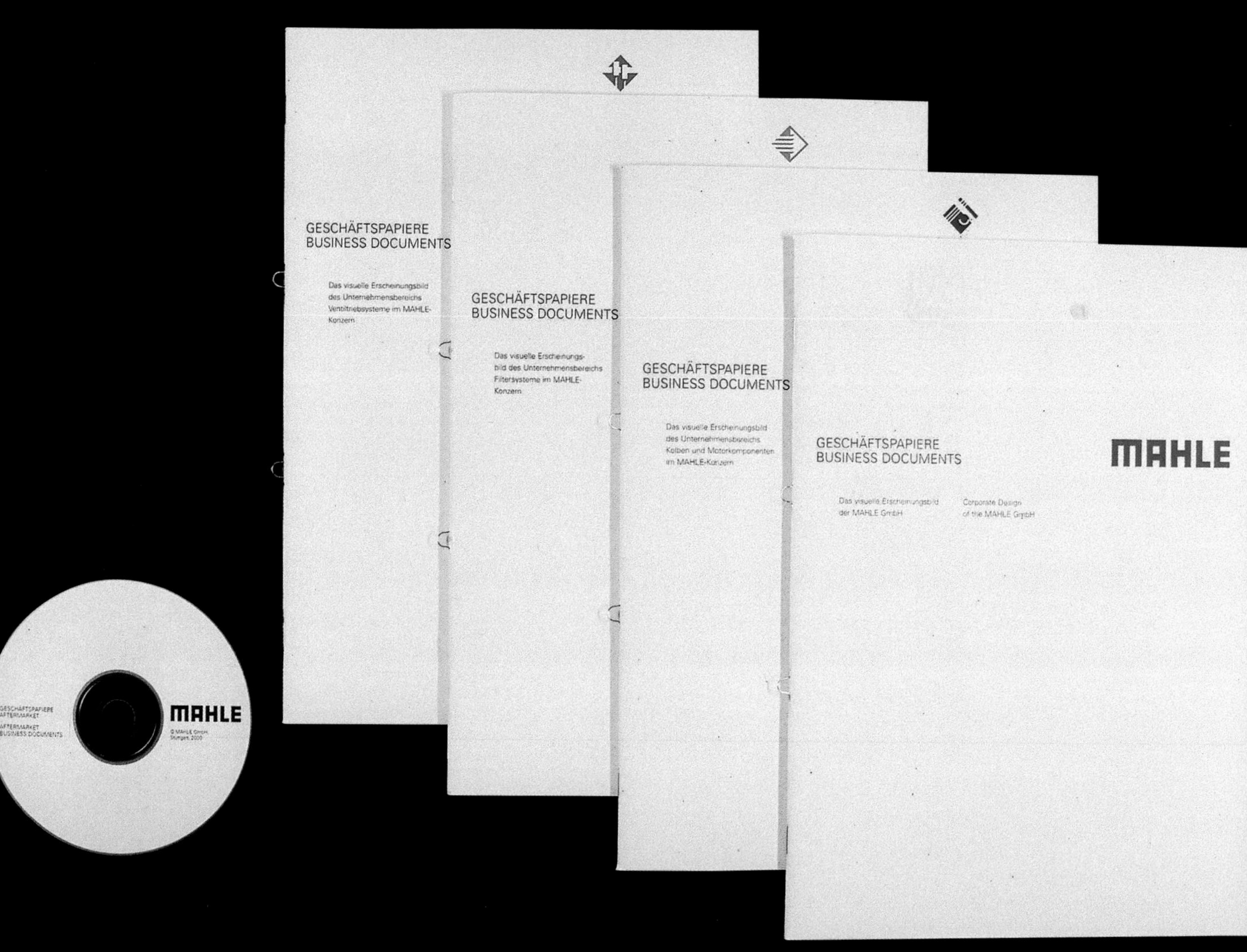

Unternehmensbereich
Kolben und
Motorkomponenten

Pistons and
Engine Components
Business Sector

Unternehmensbereich
Filtersysteme

Filter Systems
Business Sector

Unternehmensbereich
Ventiltriebsysteme

Valve Train Systems
Business Sector

Der Schriftzug beansprucht
einen Mindestfreiraum
für sich (b=1/2 Schrifthöhe)

The logo requires
a minimum amount of white
space (b=1/2 letter height)

Überarbeiteter Schriftzug
Redesigned logo

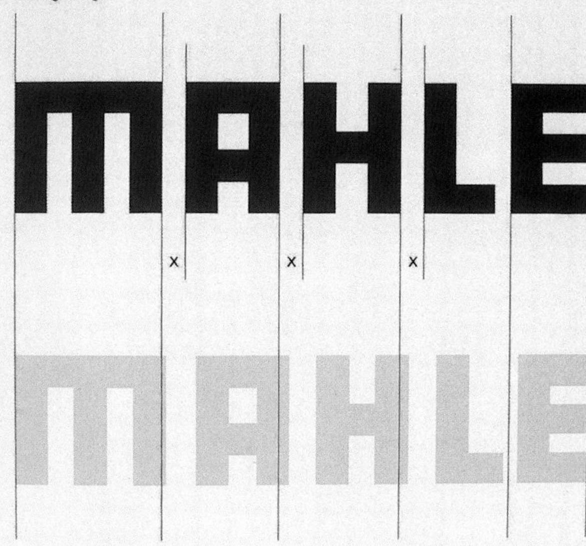

Bisheriger Schriftzug
Previous logo

Univers 45 28 pt

ABCDEFGHIJKLM
NOPQRSTUVXYZ
abcdefghijkl
mnopqrstuvwxyzä
1234567890
(.;:„"!?)

gly

Univers 55 260 pt

Univers 45 10 pt

Dieser Blindtext ist gesetzt aus der Univers 45 in zehn Punkt Größe, vierzehn Punkt Zeilenabstand. Die Schrift verfügt über zahlreiche Schnitte.

Univers 55 10 pt

This sample copy is set in Univers 55 in 10-point type with 14 points leading. This typeface has many different versions.

MAHLE-Schriftzug und Unternehmensbereich Kolben und Motorkomponenten

MAHLE Logo and Pistons and Engine Components Business Sector

Pantone 294
100% Cyan 60% Magenta 30% Black
RAL 5005

Unternehmensbereich
Filtersysteme

Filter Systems
Business Sector

Pantone 165 (HKS 8)
70% Magenta 100% Yellow
RAL 2004

Unternehmensbereich
Ventiltriebsysteme

Valve Train Systems
Business Sector

Pantone Process Magenta
100% Magenta
RAL 4010

Textfarbe
Text color

Pantone Black
100% Black
RAL 9005

Zusatzfarbe Silber für Auszeichnungen oder als Fond

Silver as additional color for emphasis or as background

Pantone 877
RAL 9006

In Sonderfällen kann Grau verwendet werden, 30% Black

Gray may be used in special cases: 30% Black

KOLBEN UND
MOTORKOMPONENTEN

MAHLE

Einladung/Invitation
IAA Frankfurt am Main
16.-26.9.1999

FILTERSYSTEME

MAHLE

Einladung/Invitation
IAA Frankfurt am Main
16.-26.9.1999

VENTILTRIEBSYSTEME

MAHLE

Einladung/Invitation
IAA Frankfurt am Main
16.-26.9.1999

Total Quality Management – Prozesssicherheit durch konsequentes Qualitätsmanagement
Qualitätsarbeit – Innovative Simulationsprogramme
Teamwork – Verkettete Materialflusskonzepte
International – MAHLE-Qualitätsnormen eingeführt
QUALITÄTSMANAGEMENT
ANNUAL REPORT
1998
MAHLE
ANNUAL REPORT
2000
MAHLE
MITARBEITER
Wachstum – Weltweit über 4 000 neue Mitarbeiter
Beschäftigung – Insgesamt über den Erwartungen
Zielvereinbarung – Mehr Transparenz in der Unternehmenssteuerung
Qualifizierung – Interne Weiterbildung erreicht Höchststand
Vorbild – Kommunikation als Erfolgsfaktor

(this spread) Design Firm **Integral Ruedi Baur et Associates** Creative Director **Denis Coueignoux** Art Director **Ruedi Baur** Designer **Martine Harle** Photographer **Blaise Adilon** Client **Centre Pompidou/Renzo Piano**

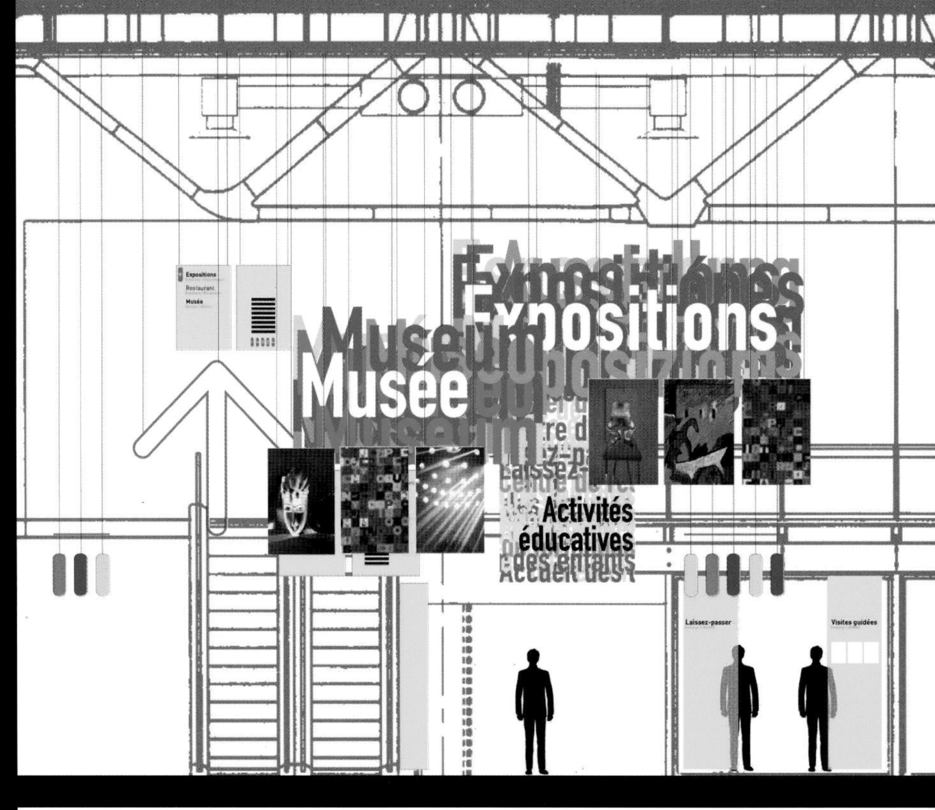

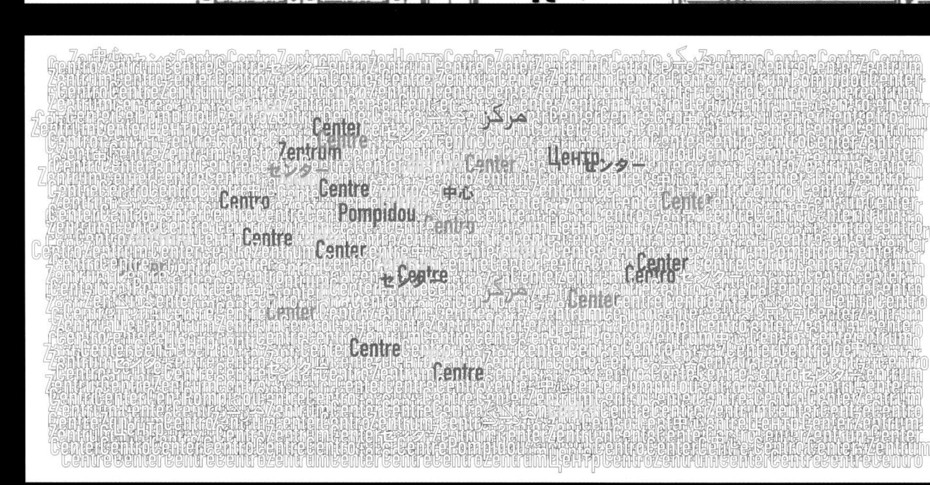

Musée
Le Temps, vite

mezzanine
Musée
The Poetics Project
Mike Kelley / Tony Oursler
Le Regard égoïste

Musée
Sortie
Atelier Brancusi
Ircam

(this spread) Design Firm **Pentagram Design** Art Director **J. Abbott Miller** Designers **J. Abbott Miller** and **Jeremy Hoffman** Client **Davis Museum and Cultural Center**

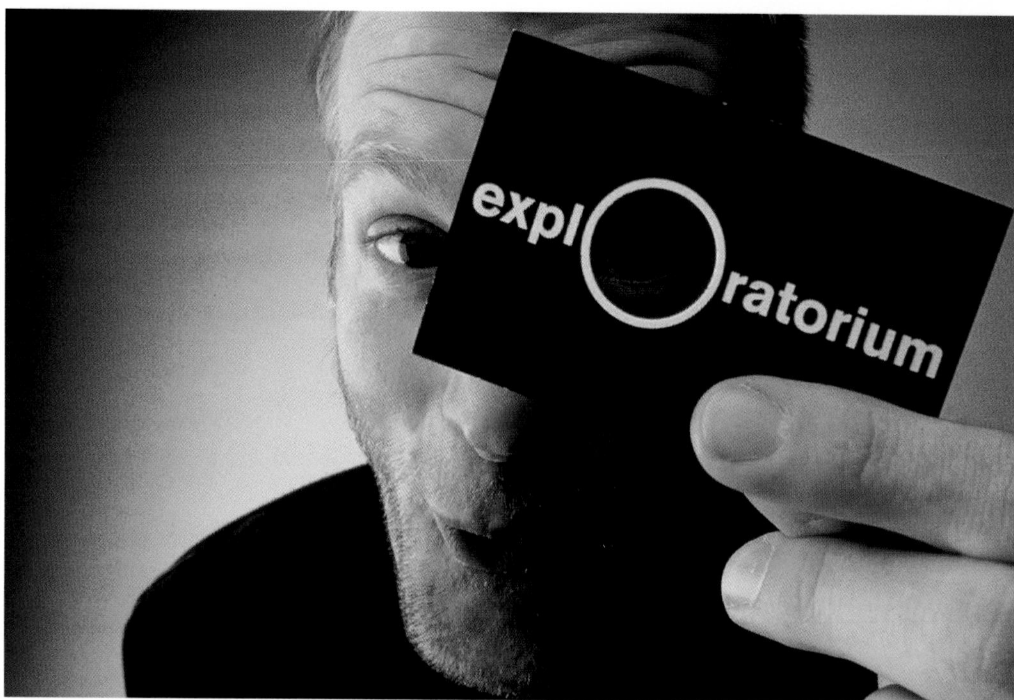

(this spread) Design Firm **Landor Associates** Creative Director **Margaret Youngblood** Designer **Douglas Sellers** Client **Exploratorium**

Exploratorium
3601 Lyon Street
San Francisco, California 94123-1019
phenomena
the museum of
science, art
and human perception
exploratorium

Exploratorium
3601 Lyon Street
San Francisco, California 94123-1019
wonder
exploratorium

Exploratorium
3601 Lyon Street
San Francisco, California 94123-1019
sense
the museum of
science, art
and human perception
exploratorium

Exploratorium
3601 Lyon Street
San Francisco, California 94123-1019
question
exploratorium

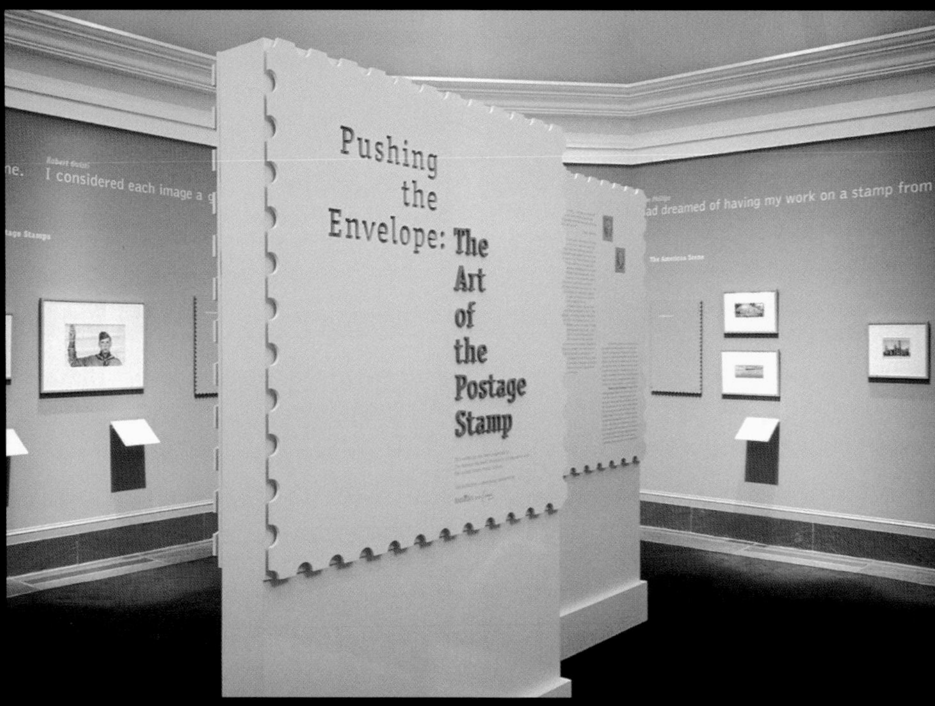

(this spread) Design Firm **Poulin & Morris** Designer **L. Richard Poulin, Jonathan Posnett** and **Shigeto Akiyama** Photographer **Tim Wilkes** Client **The Norman Rockwell Museum at Stockbridge**

(this spread) Design Firm **Pentagram Design** Creative and Art Director **Kit Hinrichs** Designer **Hizam Haron** Client **San Jose Museum of Art**

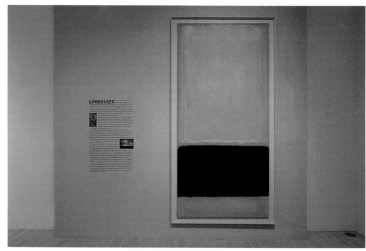

SAN JOSE MUSEUM OF ART
SAN JOSE MUSEUM OF ART
AMERICAN ART
TRADITIONS RECONSIDERED

(this spread) Design Firm **Pentagram Design** Art Director **Paula Scher** Designers **Paula Scher, Keith Daigle** and **Tina Chang** Client **New York Botanical Garden**

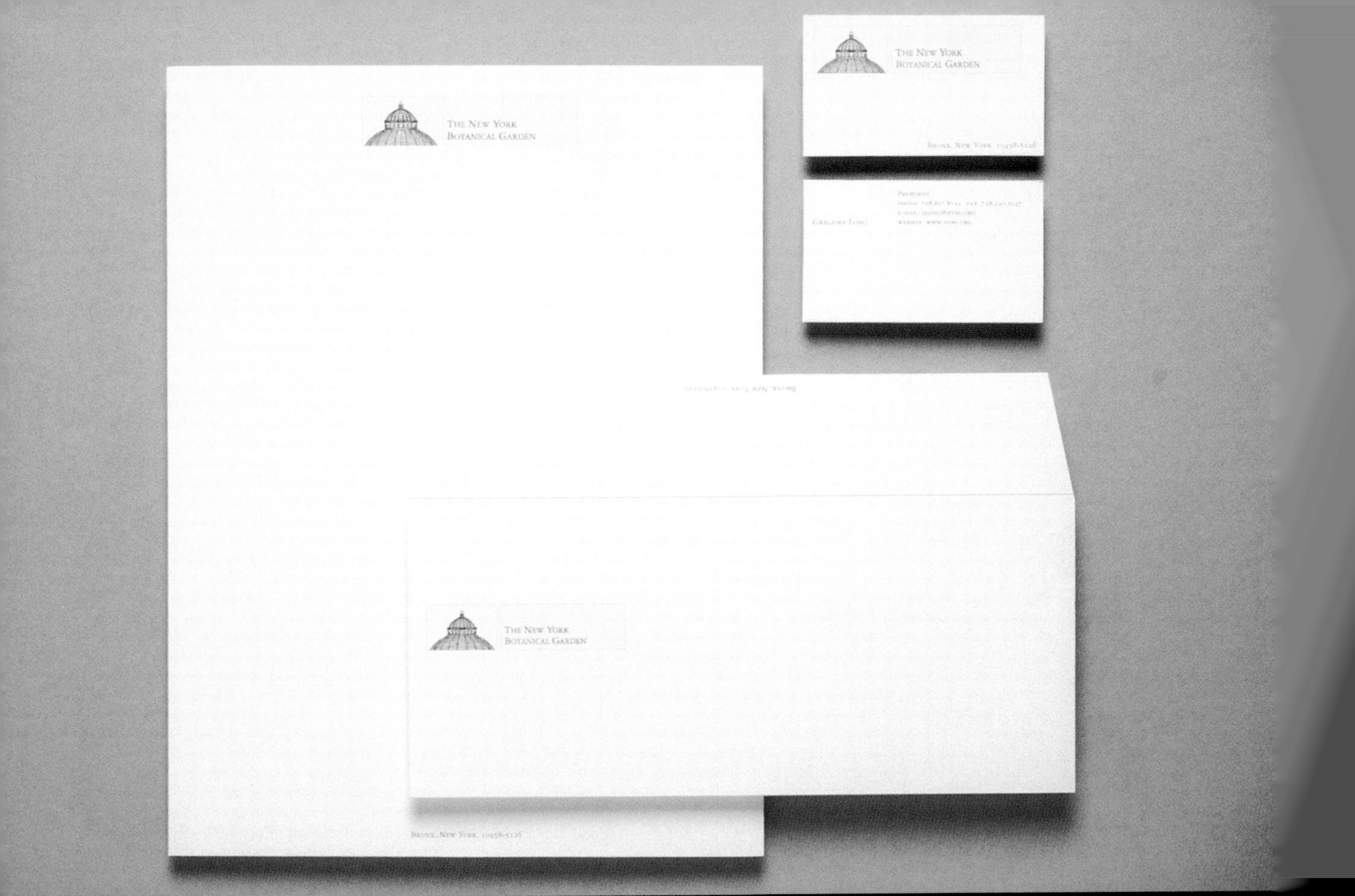

The New York
Botanical Garden

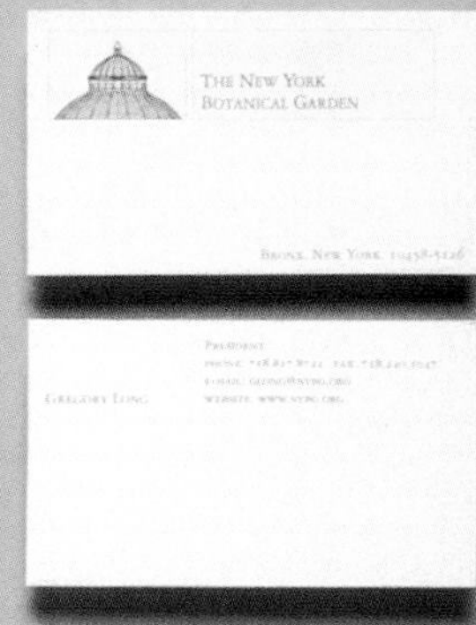
The New York
Botanical Garden
Bronx, New York, 10458-5126
President
Gregory Long

The New York
Botanical Garden

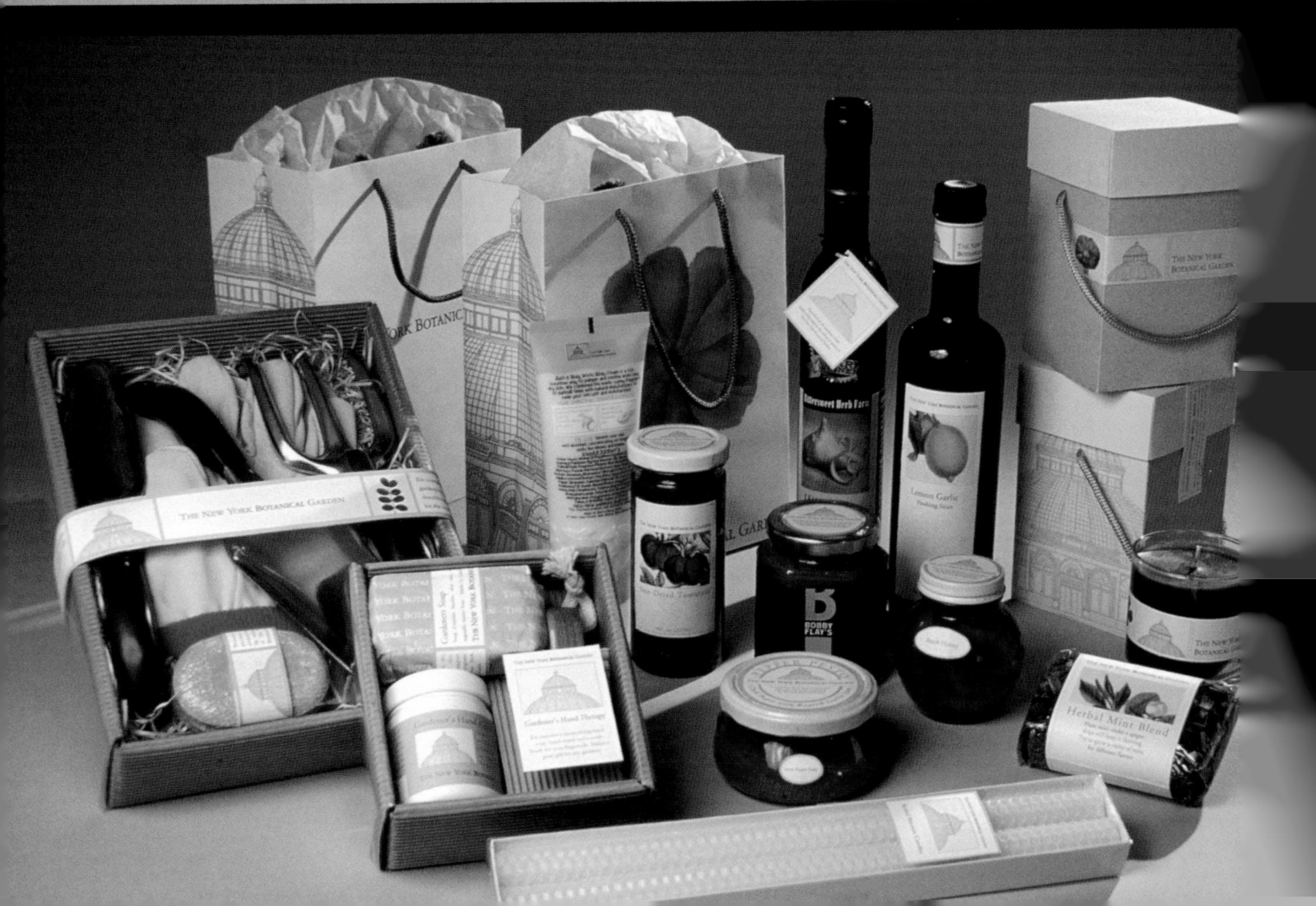

gn Firm **Supon Design Group** Creative and Art Director **Supon Phornirunlit** Designer **Lillie Fujinaga** Copywriter **Steve Smith** Client **MOCA Online**

You just spent an arm and a leg on something with no arms or legs.

Check out the value of your collectibles.

WWW.MOCAONLINE.COM

What planet is he from?

WWW.MOCAONLINE.COM

WRITE STUFF
RECYCLED KRAFT WRITING PAPER
MADE IN THE U.S.A.
12 BUSINESS SIZE ENVELOPES (#10)
24 SHEETS OF WRITING PAPER (8.5 X 11)
100% POST CONSUMER
LASER COMPATIBLE
Paper has not always been made from trees. Three hundred years ago, the first American paper mills made writing paper from old rags. In the spirit of these early recycled papers, Write Stuff is made entirely from old cardboard boxes and kraft bags. The result is an
Found Stuff PaperWorks is a micro-paper mill producing paper in the early American tradition—recycled. In the spirit of the first American mills, the Write Stuff is produced from 100% recycled post-consumer materials. In place of the cloth rags used by early mills to make fine paper, the Write Stuff is made from old cardboard boxes and kraft bags. The machine created to glue layers of paper together to make cardboard was invented in 1824. Cardboard is now the largest single grade of paper produced in the U.S. and is used worldwide for packaging and shipping products. As one of America's leading export products,
WRITE STUFF
LASER COMPATIBLE

Premium

HEMP PAPER

Another Tree Free Paper From

Green Field Paper Co.

100% RECYCLED · 70 LB/180 GSM · 40 PAGES · ACID FREE · MADE IN THE USA

GROW A NOTE

The Notecard You Plant

GREEN FIELD
PAPER COMPANY

CARROT

RADISH

EGGPLANT

LETTUCE

GROW A NOTE

WRITE IT · MAIL IT · PLANT IT ·

(this spread) Design Firm **Emerson, Wajdowicz Studios** Creative Director **Jurek Wajdowicz** Art Director **Lisa Larochelle** Designers **Jurek Wajdowicz** and **Lisa Larochelle** Client **Domtar Communication Papers**

BRAVO PINKHASSOV
BRAVO TOWELL
BRAVO WEBB
BRAVO McCURRY
BRAVO SCIANNA
BRAVO TURBEVILLE
BRAVO RICHARDS

ative Director **Scott Sample** Designer **Sean Lien** Photographer **John Mowers** Copywriter **Ruth Harvey** Client **Mowers Photography**

MOWERS PHOTOGRAPHY
JOHN E. MOWERS
MOWERS PHOTOGRAPHY
MOWERS PHOTOGRAPHY

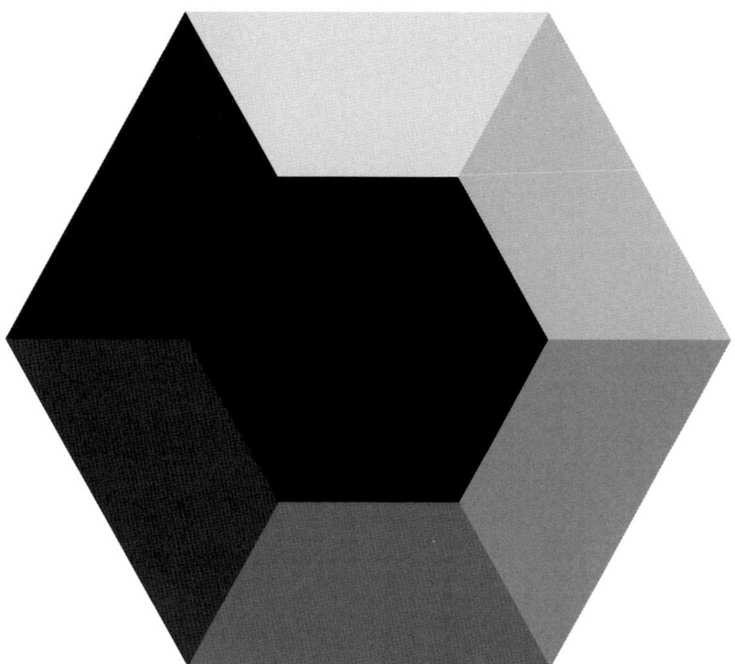

(this spread) Design Firm **ge-stolt 5** Art Director **Robert Szabo** Designers **Robert Szabo, Robert Perry** and **George Stephenson** Client **Stephenson Printing Inc.**

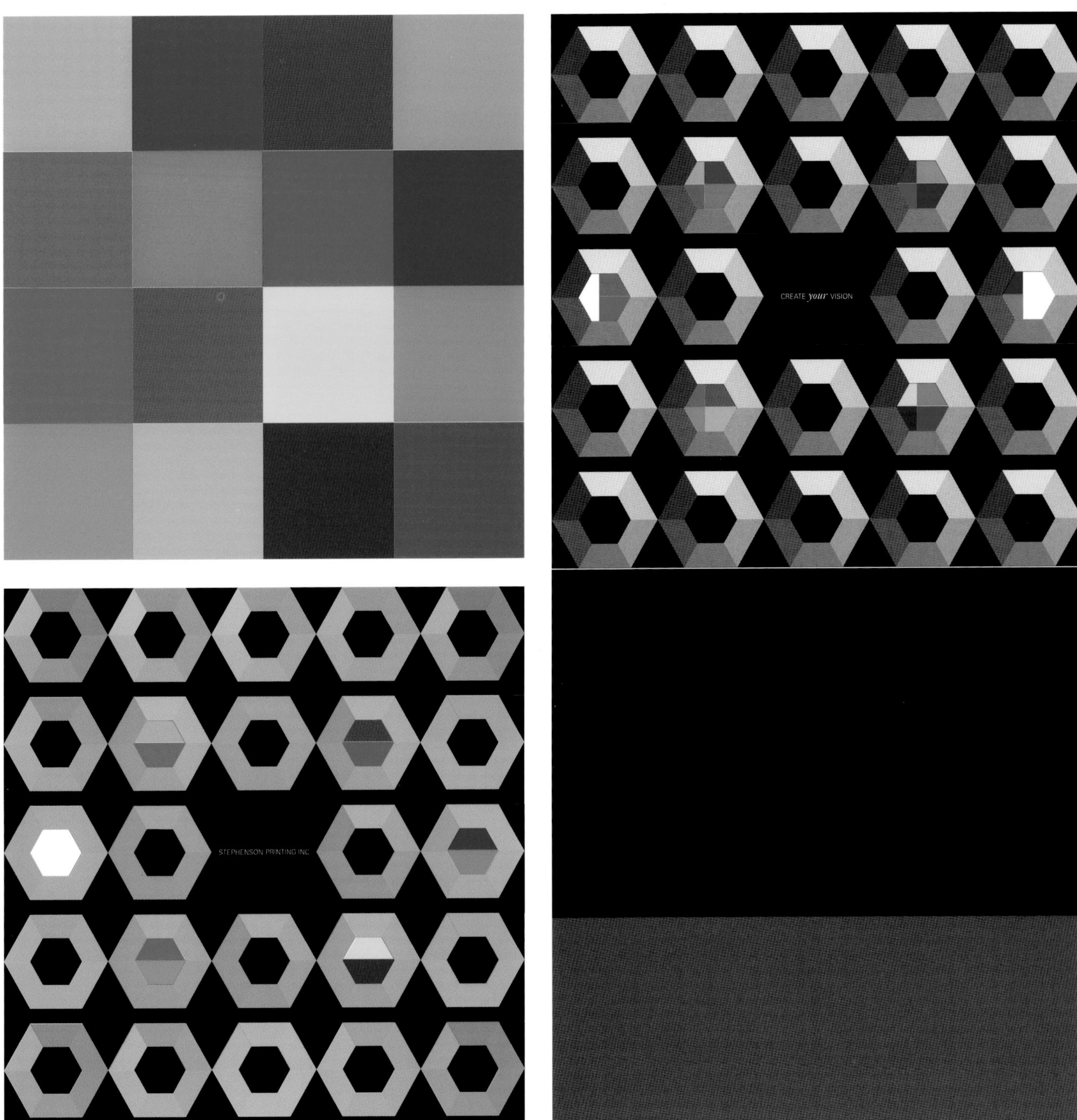
CREATE your VISION
STEPHENSON PRINTING INC.

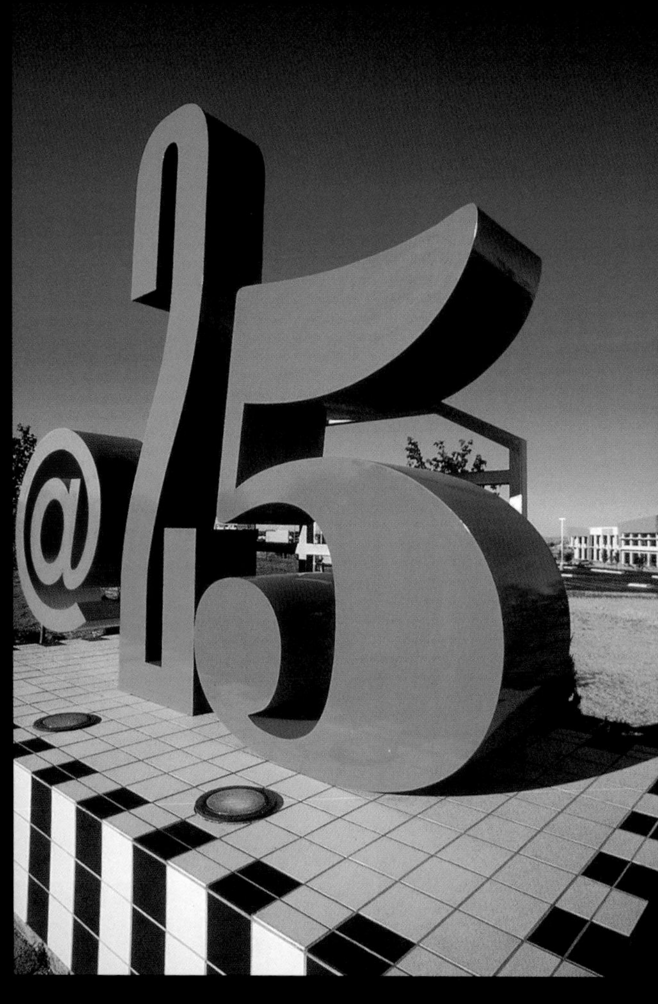

(this spread) Design Firm **Vaughn Wedeen Creative** Creative Director, Art Director and Designer **Rick Vaughn** Photographer **Michael Barley** Client **Provident Realty Advisors**

4420

CLIENTLOGIC

Furr's
SUPERMARKETS

(this spread) Design Firm **Graphics and Designing Inc.** Art Director and Designer **Toshihiro Onimaru** Client **New York Cafe**

NEW YORK CAFE
NYC
NEW YORK CAFE
COFFEE
Junji Kono
Director
2F MA-Bldg.
Nishi6Minami1,
Chuo-ku,Sapporo
#060-0061 Japan.
Tel.011-252-2249
2F MA-Bldg,Nishi6-Minami1,Chuo-ku,Sapporo 060-0061 Japan. Tel.011-252-2249

(this and following spread) Design Firm **Love the Life** Creative Directors, Art Directors and Designers **Akemi Katsuno** and **Takashi Yagi** Wall Art **Shie Kutsuna** Display Design **Aki Ito** Client **Move Co.**

kranz

kranz
kranz
kranz

P
ホール・会議室
780-0008

spread) Design Firm **Alan Chan Design Co.** Creative and Art Director **Alan Chan** Designers **Alan Chan, Alvin Chan, Miu Choy** and **Polly Ko** Client **Kee Wah Ltd. Hong Kong**

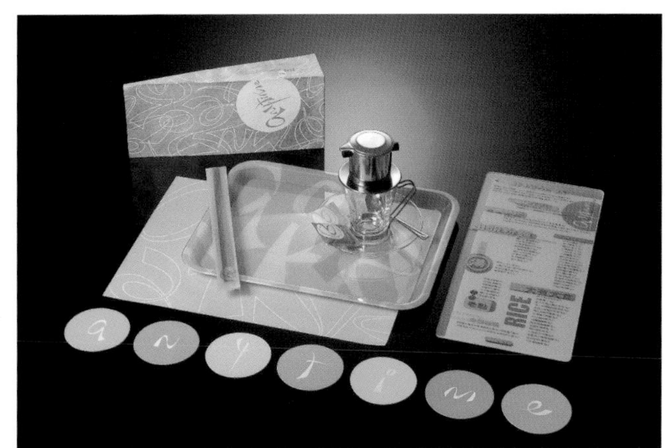

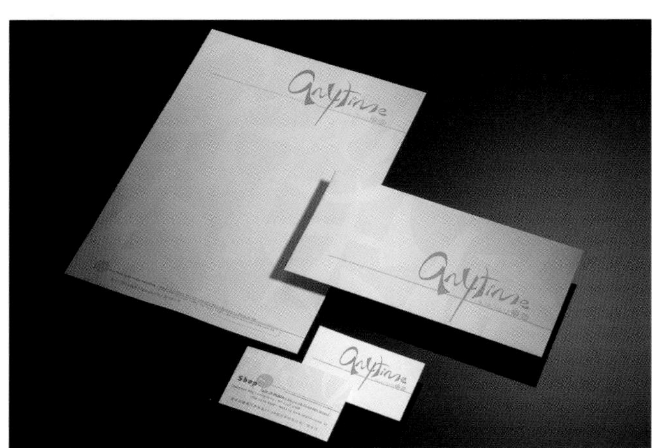

(this spread) Design Firm **Sayles Graphic Design** Creative Director, Art Director and Designer **John Sayles** Photographer **Bill Nellans** Client **Mezzodi's**

KNOB
CREEK

Pâtes
BARONI

(this spread) Design Firm **Zenaro GmbH, Architekur und Design** Art Directors **Markus Huber** and **Michel Nigg** Photographers **Marco Blessano** and **Markus Huber** Copywriter **Patrick Thomann** Client **Blue Steel Music Bar**

CALIENTE
COFFEE
GATTI'S
FRESH

S U P R E M O
SALADS
GATTI'S
g
FRESH
MR. GATTI'S SALAD INGREDIENTS ARE SO FRESH YOU MAY HAVE TO SLAP THEM.

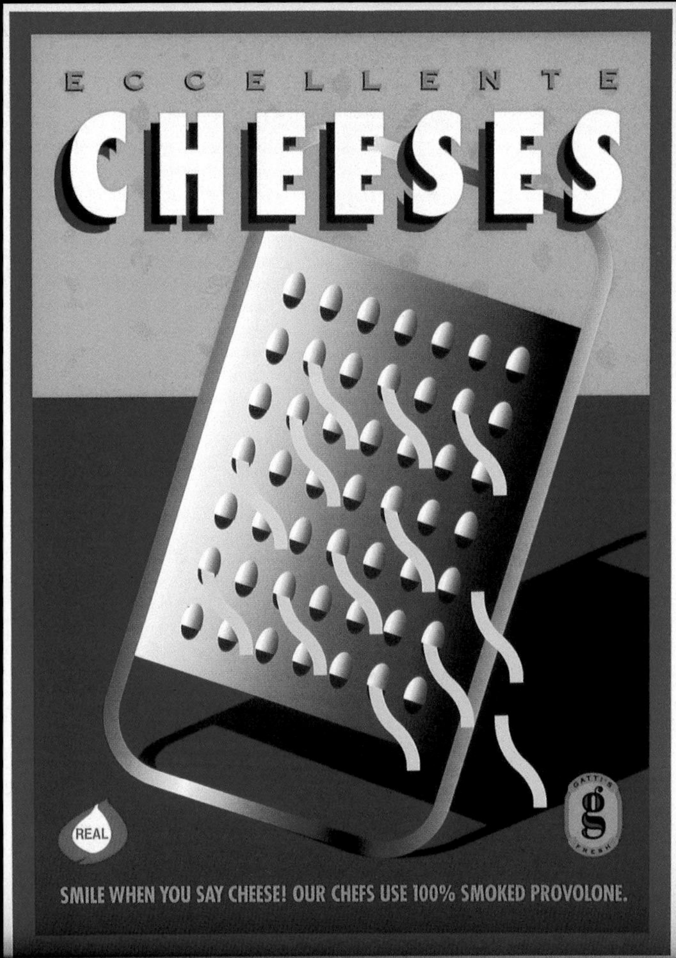
E C C E L L E N T E
CHEESES
REAL
GATTI'S
g
FRESH
SMILE WHEN YOU SAY CHEESE! OUR CHEFS USE 100% SMOKED PROVOLONE.

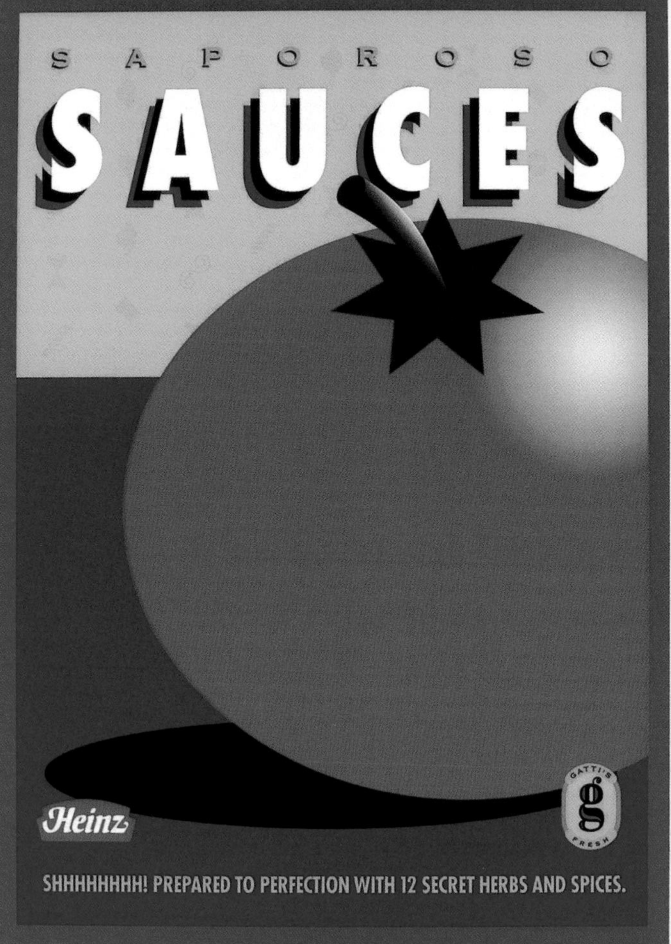
S A P O R O S O
SAUCES
Heinz
GATTI'S
g
FRESH
SHHHHHHHH! PREPARED TO PERFECTION WITH 12 SECRET HERBS AND SPICES.

D E L I Z I O S O
DRINKS
Coca-Cola
Coca-Cola
GATTI'S
g
FRESH
WE'RE POURING ON THE REFRESHMENT WITH THE COLDEST DRINKS IN TOWN.

(this spread) Design Firm **Duffy Design and Interactive** Creative Director **Joe Duffy** Art Director **Kobe Suvongse** Designers **Kobe Suvongse, Craig Duffney, Tom Kelley** and **Ron Gallas** Photographer **Dana Wheelock** Illustrators **Kobe Suvongse, Craig Duffney, Jim Holmberg, Dan Michiel, Andy Powell** and **Leon Huscha** Client **Zelo (Rick Webb Restaurants)**

(this spread) Design Firm **Sayles Graphic Design** Creative Director, Art Director and Designer **John Sayles** Photographer **Bill Nellans** Client **Phil Goode Grocery**

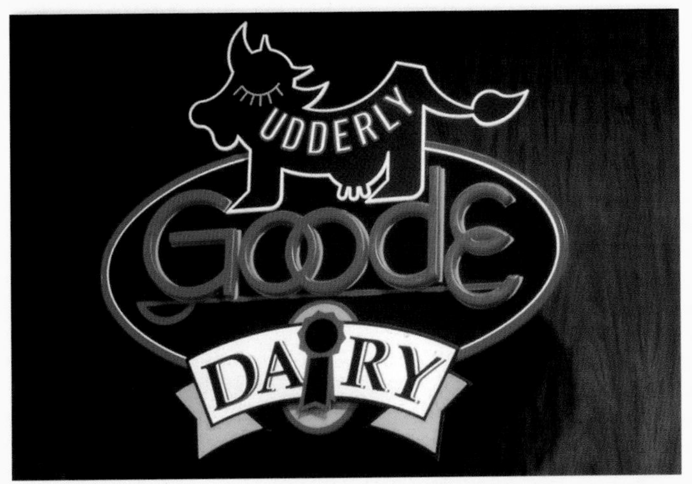
UDDERLY
GOODE
DAIRY

SQUEEZED
GOODE
Juice

GOODE
GRINDE™
COFFEE

PHIL
GOODE
GROCERY™

COLD
GOODE
SODA

-0°
GOODE
N
COLDER

(this spread) Design Firm **Graphics and Designing Inc.** Art Director and Designer **Toshihiro Onimaru** Client **George's Furniture Co. Ltd.**

GEORGE'S

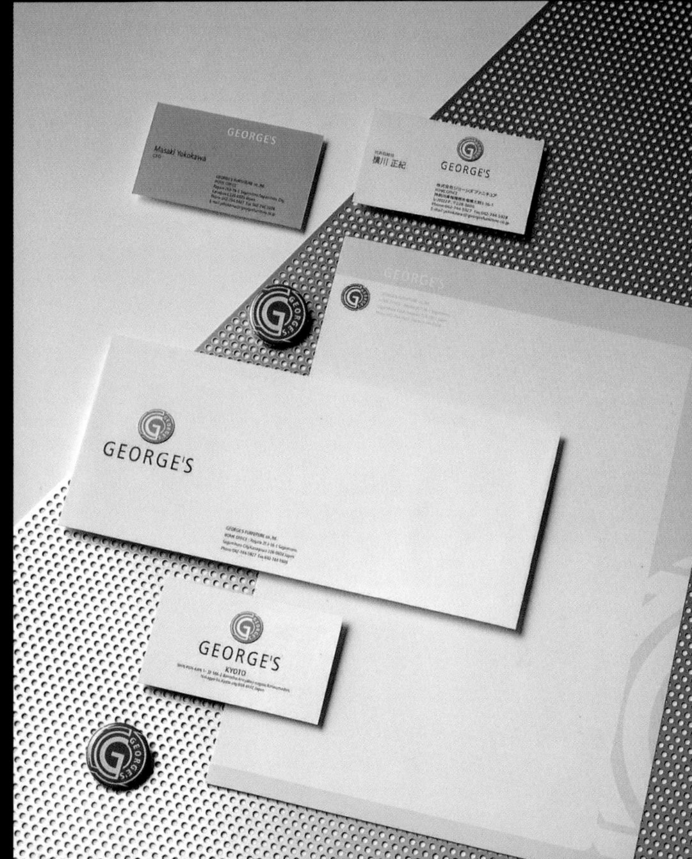
GEORGE'S
Misaki Yokokawa
GEORGE'S
KYOTO

GEORGE'S

GEORGE'S

(this spread) Design Firm **Love the Life** Creative Directors, Art Directors and Designers **Akemi Katsuno** and **Takashi Yagi** Client **Thirty Three Co. Ltd.**

SHOP 2

flowers
TOMMY LUKE

PEARL DISTRICT 1225 NW EVERETT PORTLAND OREGON 97209 228·3140

(this spread) Design Firm **Sandstrom Design** Creative Director, Art Director and Designer **Steve Sandstrom** Production Designer **Starlee Matz** Photographer **Paul Foster** Client **Flowers Tommy Luke**

flowers
TOMMY LUKE
1225 N.W. EVERETT, PORTLAND, OREGON 97209
phone 503.228.3140 fax 503.778.5544
FLOWERS
flowers
TOMMY LUKE
FLORA YUEN
1225 N.W. EVERETT, PORTLAND, OREGON 97209
phone 503.228.3140 fax 503.778.5544
flowers
TOMMY LUKE
FLORAL DESIGN BY
Linda Bill
flowers
TOMMY LUKE
flowers
TOMMY LUKE

(this spread) Design Firm **Duffy Design and Interactive** Creative Director **Joe Duffy** Art Director **Kobe Suvongse** Designers **Kobe Suvongse, Jason Strong** and **Dan Olson** Photographer **Dana Wheelock** Copywriters **Mary Senn** and **Lisa Pemerick** Client **Retail Concepts**

FIRST
TRADE MARK
BASIN
MPLS./ST. PAUL
BEST

MOISTURIZER
MOUSSE
SLATHER

FIRST
TRADE MARK
BASIN
PAUL
BUBBLERS
Effervescent bubbles & soul-soothing scents
turn bathing into fizzical therapy.

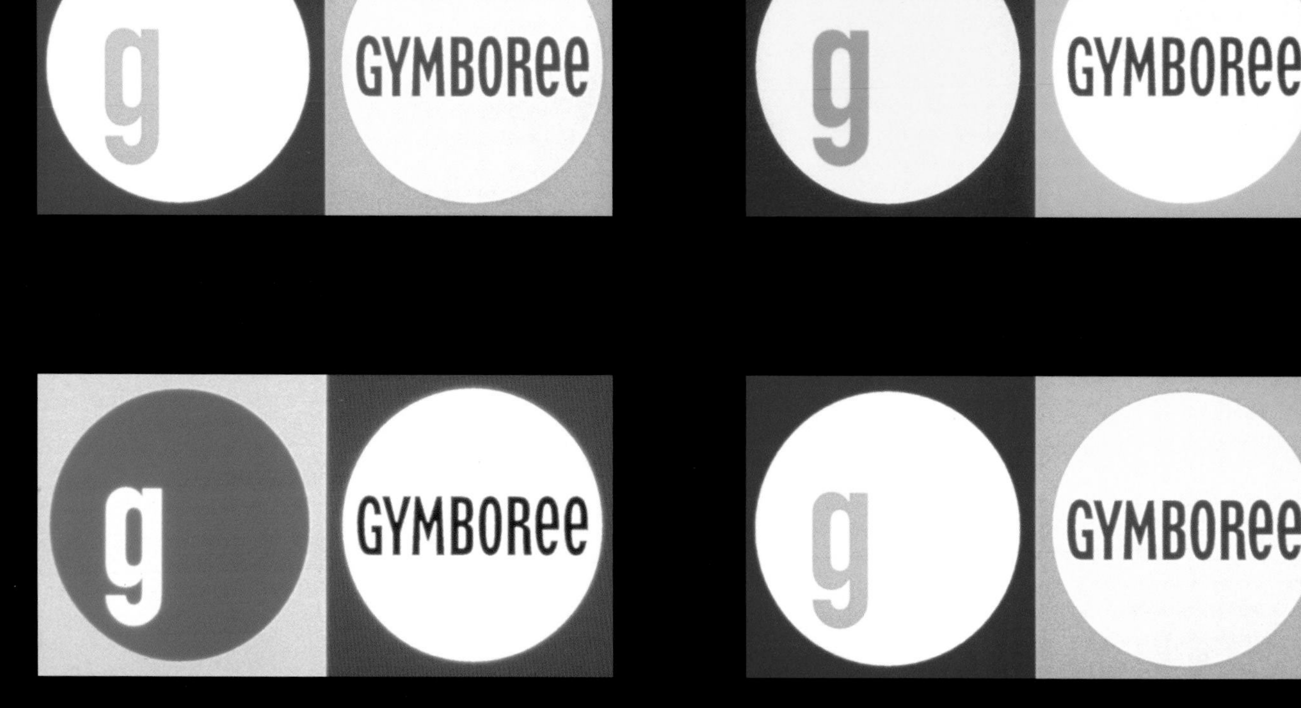

Design Firm **Michael Osborne Design** Art Director **Michael Osborne** Designer **Paul Kagiwada** Client **Gymboree**

GYMBOREE
www.gymboree.com
3-12 mos.

spread) Design Firm **Sandstrom Design** Creative Director **Steve Sandstrom** Art Director and Designer **Jon Olsen** Production Designer **Starlee Matz** Illustrator **Larry Jost** Copywriter **Leslee Dillon** Client **Castor & Pollux**

CASTOR & POLLUX
PAW
MADE
"WE MAKE STUFF WE LIKE"
CURIOUS CAT
ORGANIC CATNIP TOY
ALL NATURAL
GOOD BUDDY
COOKIES
OUT SPOT
GOTTA GO
KITTY LITTER
PLAY DEAD
HERBAL COLLAR
PRESSED
"Treat your pet right."

(this spread) Design Firm **Morla Design** Creative Director **Brian Coffins** Art Director **Jennifer Morla** Designers **Jennifer Morla, Ann Culbertson** and **Gaby Brink** Photographer **Cesar Rubio** Copywriter **Brian Collins** Client **Foote, Cone & Belding/Levi Strauss & Co.**

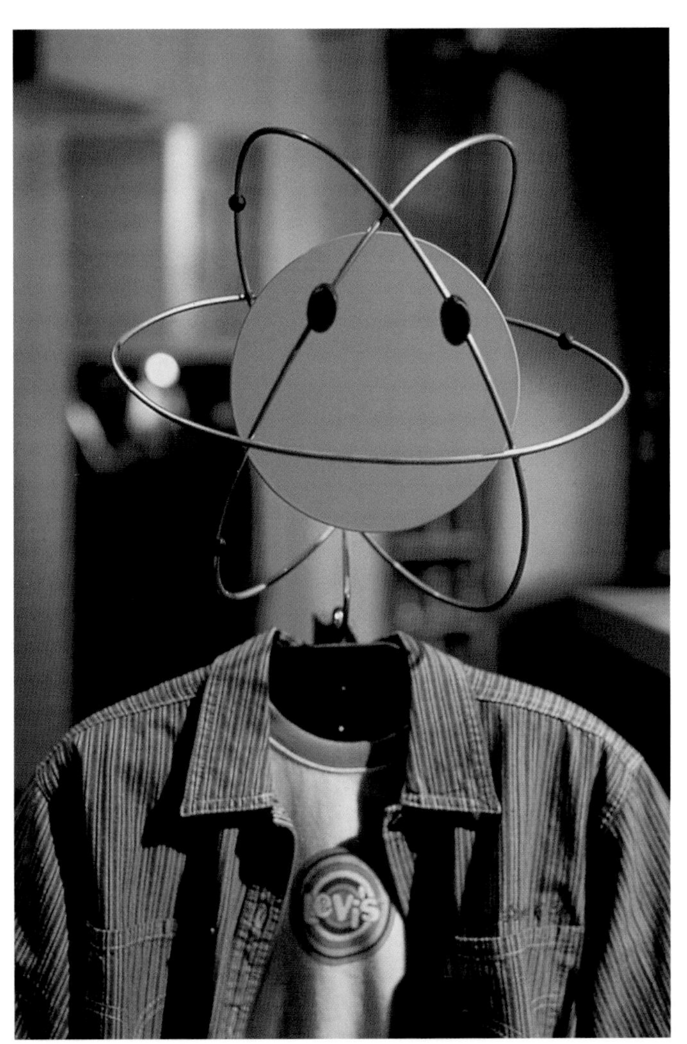
Levi's

Levi's
550
550
501
LAB
RESEARCH
STYLE
LAB: LEVI'S

LEVI'S

(this spread) Design Firm **The Leonhardt Group** with **Corbin Design** Designers **Mark Popich** and **Robert Brengman** Client **REI**

REI

To Store Entrance
To John Street
To Bus Stop
Cycle Test Trail

Women

To Store
P1 P1

Climbing
Camping
Cashiers
Sale

(this spread) Design Firm **Pentagram Design Ltd.** Art Director **David Hillman** Designer **Simon Pickford** Client **Time Products**

MARCUS
MARCUS

(this spread) Design Firm **Duffy Design and Interactive** Creative and Art Director **Alan Colvin** Designers **Alan Colvin, Ken Sakurai** and **Craig Duffney** Photographer **Richard Klein** Illustrators **Alan Colvin, Ken Sakurai** and **Craig Duffney** Client **Nordstrom**

NORDSTR
Drinks
ESPRESSO MAKES YOU VERY VERY AWAKE
WATER
COFFEE BAR

house

CAFE AND COFFEE BAR

CAFE AND COFFEE BAR

(this spread) Design Firm **North Castle Design** Creative Director **Rudy Mossa** Designers **John Ferris** and **Mike Callahan** Client **Tomra of North America**

re PLANET
Recycling Center
7am - 11pm
Machines
7am - 11pm
Machines
Recycling Center

OSAKA
2008
OSAKA
2008
CANDIDATE CITY

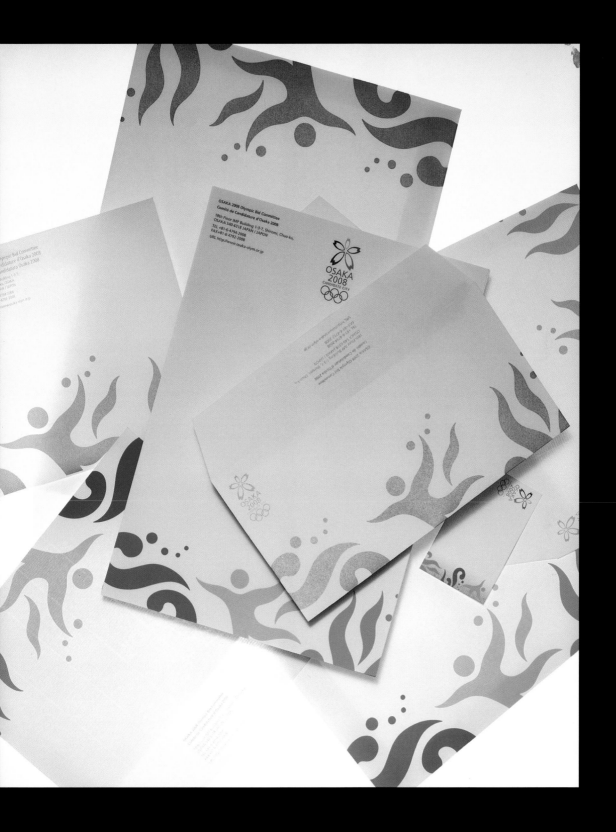

(this and following spread) Design Firm **FHA Image Design** Creative Director, Art Director, Designer, Photographer and Illustrator **FHA Image Design** Client **Sydney Organizing Committee for the Olympic Games**

OSAKA 2008 BID EMBLEM

09
エンブレム

公式エンブレムには、SOLIDタイプとINTERLOCKINGタイプがあります。
五輪の幅が1cm以内の場合は、必ずSOLIDタイプを使用します。

公式エンブレム SOLIDタイプ

公式エンブレム INTERLOCKINGタイプ

清刷 SOLIDタイプ

清刷 INTERLOCKINGタイプ

APPLICATIONS

14-1
展開例 ポスター

CHART

05-1
カラー展開

Single

Combination

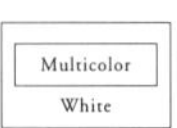

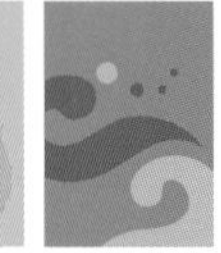

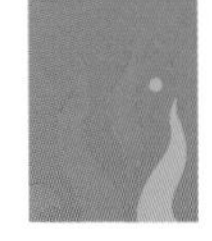
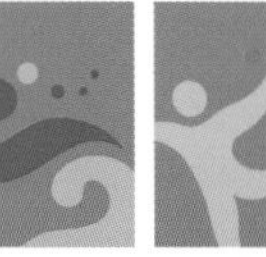
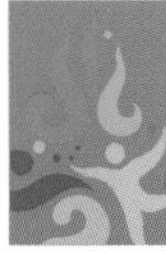

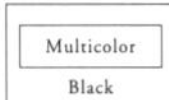

TYPOGRAPHY

08
使用書体

サブグラフィックを使って展開したデザインでは、イメージの統一を図るため以下の書体を使用します。

Adobe Garamond Regular

ABCDEFGHIJKLMNOPQRSTUVWXYZ
abcdefghijklmnopqrstuvwxyz&,.1234567890

Adobe Garamond Bold

ABCDEFGHIJKLMNOPQRSTUVWXYZ
abcdefghijklmnopqrstuvwxyz&,.1234567890

Frutiger Roman

ABCDEFGHIJKLMNOPQRSTUVWXYZ
abcdefghijklmnopqrstuvwxyz&,.1234567890

Frutiger Bold

ABCDEFGHIJKLMNOPQRSTUVWXYZ
abcdefghijklmnopqrstuvwxyz&,.1234567890

Title

OSAKA 2008

OSAKA 2008

III

OSAKA 2008

I

OSAKA 2008

II

Cafe
Geo
19

3

Old Well
EXIT
FIRE
FIRE

spread) Design Firm **FHA Image Design** Creative Director, Art Director, Designer, Photographer and Illustrator **FHA Image Design** Architect **Lahz Nimmo** Client **Sydney Organizing Committee for the Olympic Games**

Live
Balmoral Park
Olympics
Live
ENTRANCE TO
NTRAL STATIO
TAXIS
AND ALL OTHER VEHICL
TT ST AND RAILWAY SQ
Sydney 2000

(this spread) Design Firm **Pentagram Design** Art Director **Michael Bierut** Designers **Michael Bierut, Karen Parolek** and **Bob Stern** Client **Brooklyn Academy of Music**

Tick
Up

(this spread) Design Firm **Pentagram Design** Art Director **Paula Scher** Designers **Paula Scher** and **Anke Stohlmann** Client **The Public Theater**

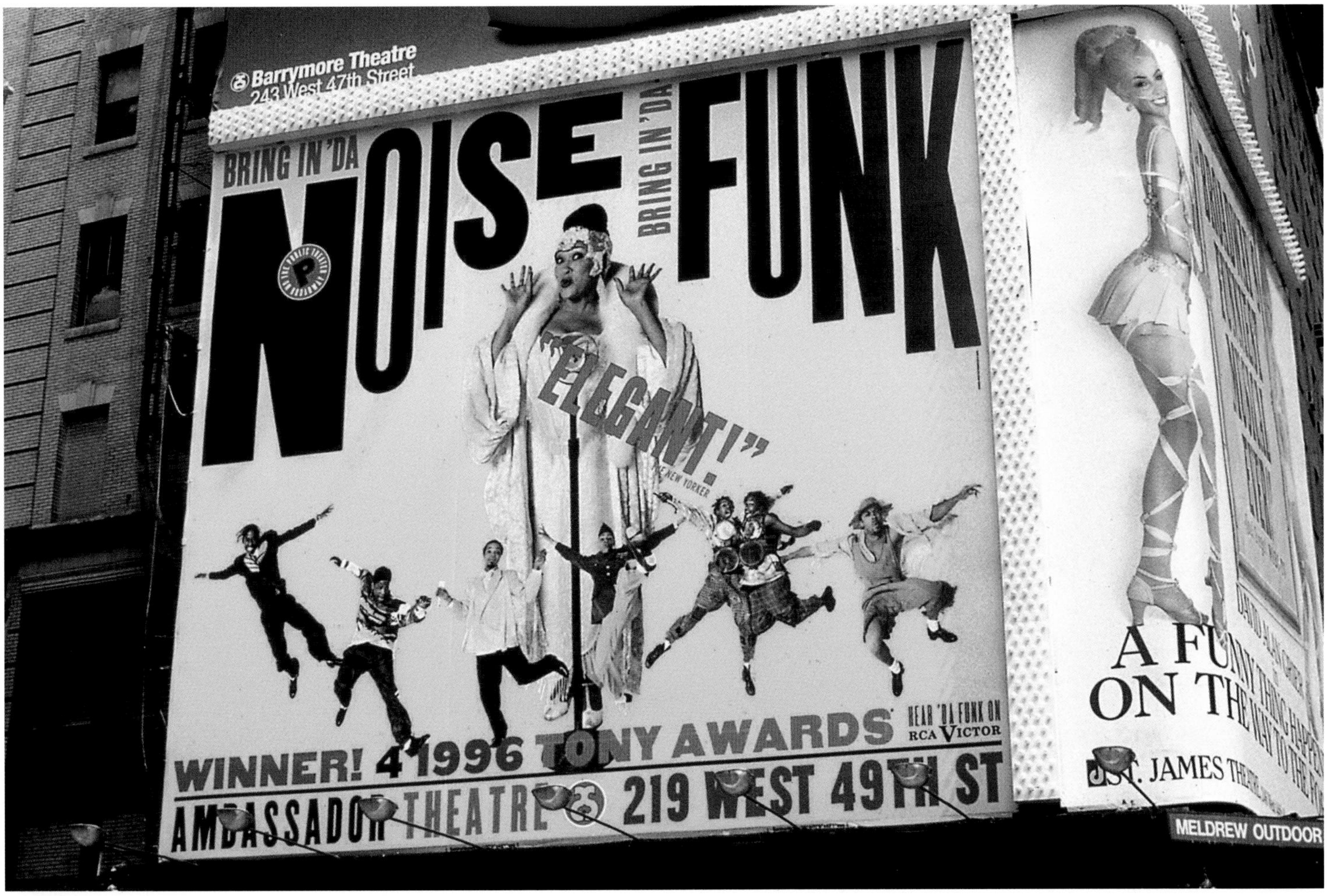

Barrymore Theatre
243 West 47th Street
BRING IN 'DA
NOISE
BRING IN 'DA
FUNK
"ELEGANT!"
THE NEW YORKER
HEAR 'DA FUNK ON
RCA VICTOR
WINNER! 4 1996 TONY AWARDS
AMBASSADOR THEATRE
219 WEST 49TH ST
A FUNNY THING HAPPENED
ON THE WAY TO THE FORUM
ST. JAMES THEATRE
MELDREW OUTDOOR

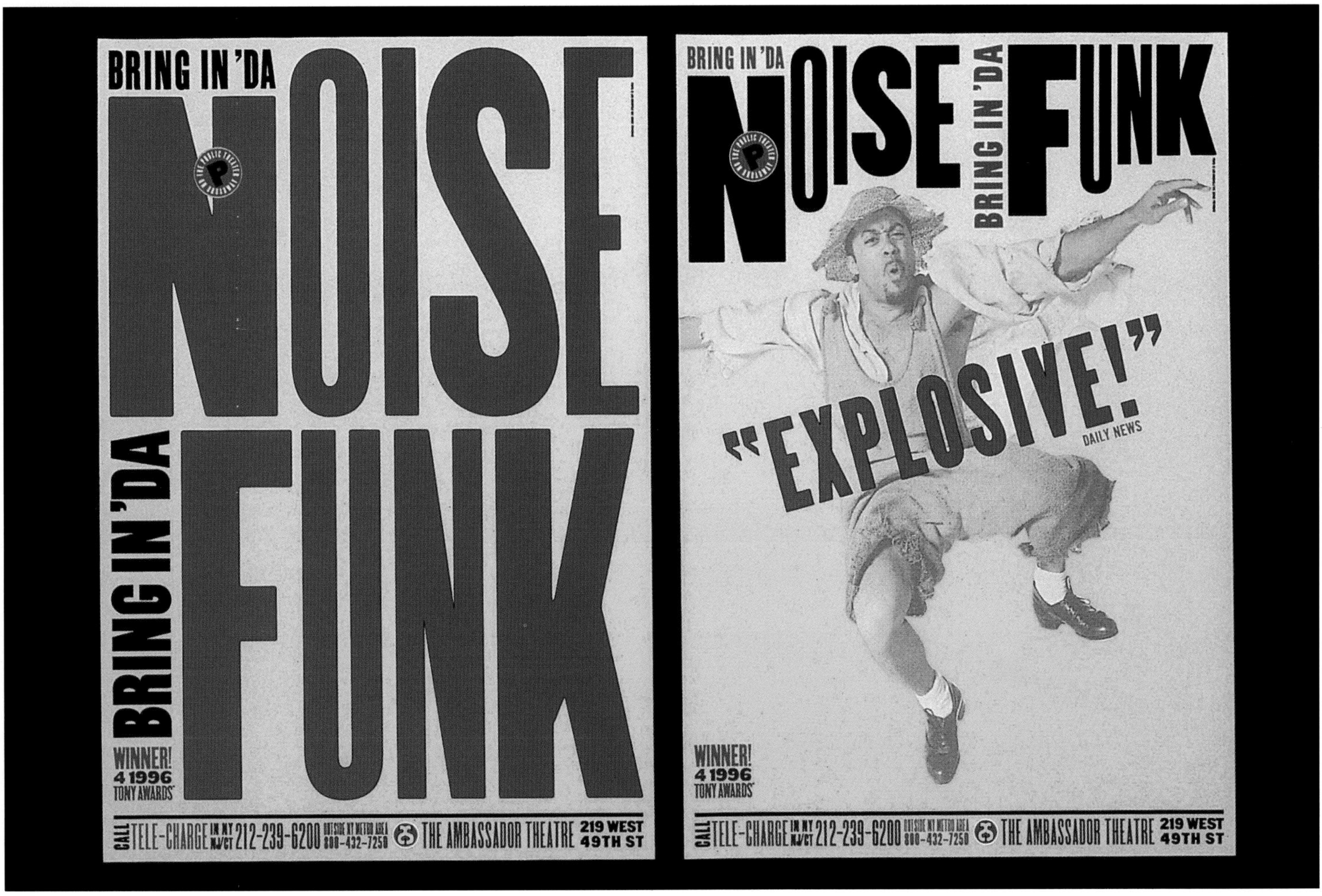

BRING IN 'DA
NOISE
BRING IN 'DA
FUNK
WINNER!
4 1996
TONY AWARDS
CALL TELE-CHARGE IN NY NJ/CT 212-239-6200 OUTSIDE NY METRO AREA 800-432-7250
THE AMBASSADOR THEATRE
219 WEST 49TH ST
BRING IN 'DA
NOISE
BRING IN 'DA
FUNK
"EXPLOSIVE!"
DAILY NEWS
WINNER!
4 1996
TONY AWARDS
CALL TELE-CHARGE IN NY NJ/CT 212-239-6200 OUTSIDE NY METRO AREA 800-432-7250
THE AMBASSADOR THEATRE
219 WEST 49TH ST

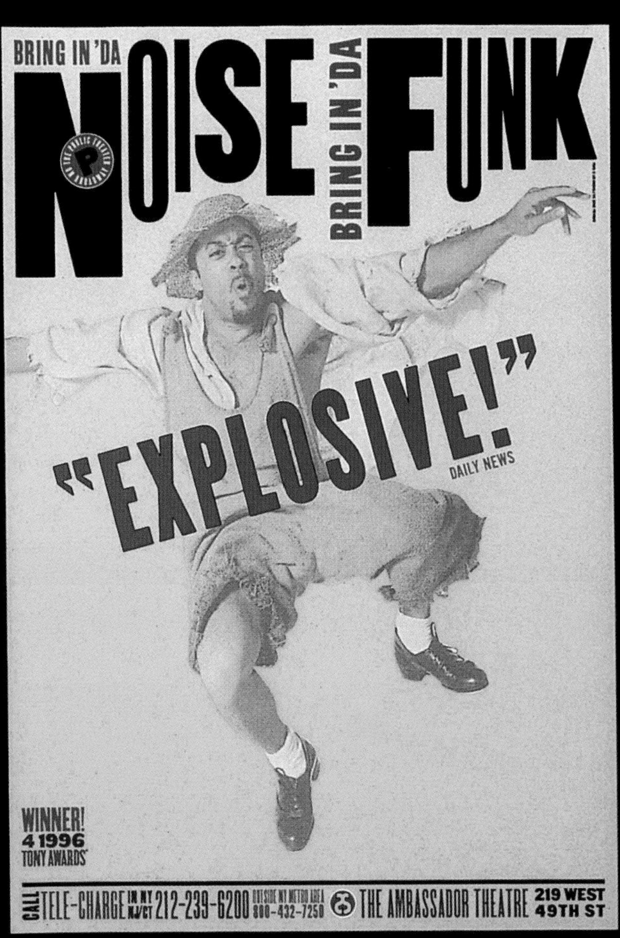

Landor Associates Creative Directors **Courtney Reeser** and **Scott Drummond** Design Directors **David Zapata** and **Paul Chock** Designers **Ivan Thelin, Keri Findlay, Joanna Bianchi** and **Todd True** Client **Canadian Airlines**

Canadian

Canadian
oneworld

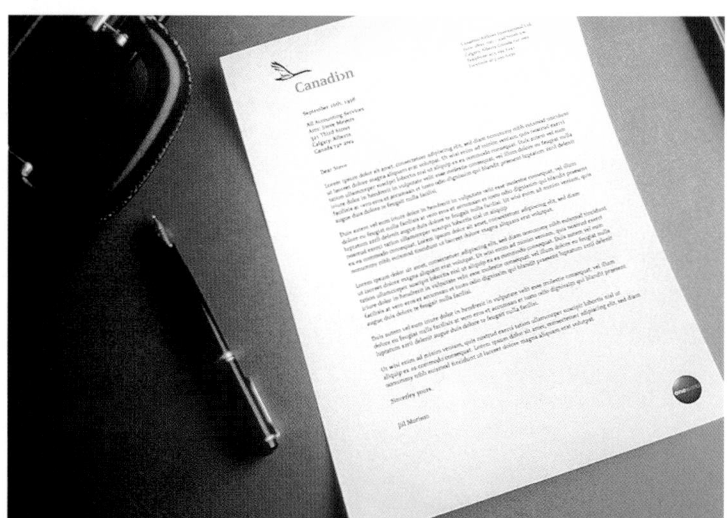
Canadian

Canadian

C-GMWW
Canadian

Canadian

5
7
9
Ground
Shuttle
Door-To-
Vans

(this spread) Design Firm **Skidmore Owings & Merrill LLP** Designers **Lonny Israel, Erin O'Reilly** and **Craig Hartman** Photographer **Tim Hursley** Client **San Francisco International Airport**

Design Firm **Selbert Perkins Design** Design Director **Nick Groh** Art Directors **Robin Perkins** and **Cliff Selbert** Designer **Clint Woesner** Client **Los Angeles World Airport**

Index Verzeichnisse Indices

CreativeDirectorsArtDirectorsDesigners

CreativeDirectorsArtDirectorsDesigners

Design Firms

PhotographersIllustrators

Copywriters

Clients

Clients

Graphis331
GLASER/FROST DESIGN/CURIOSITY/SIROTA/KESSELSKRAMER/

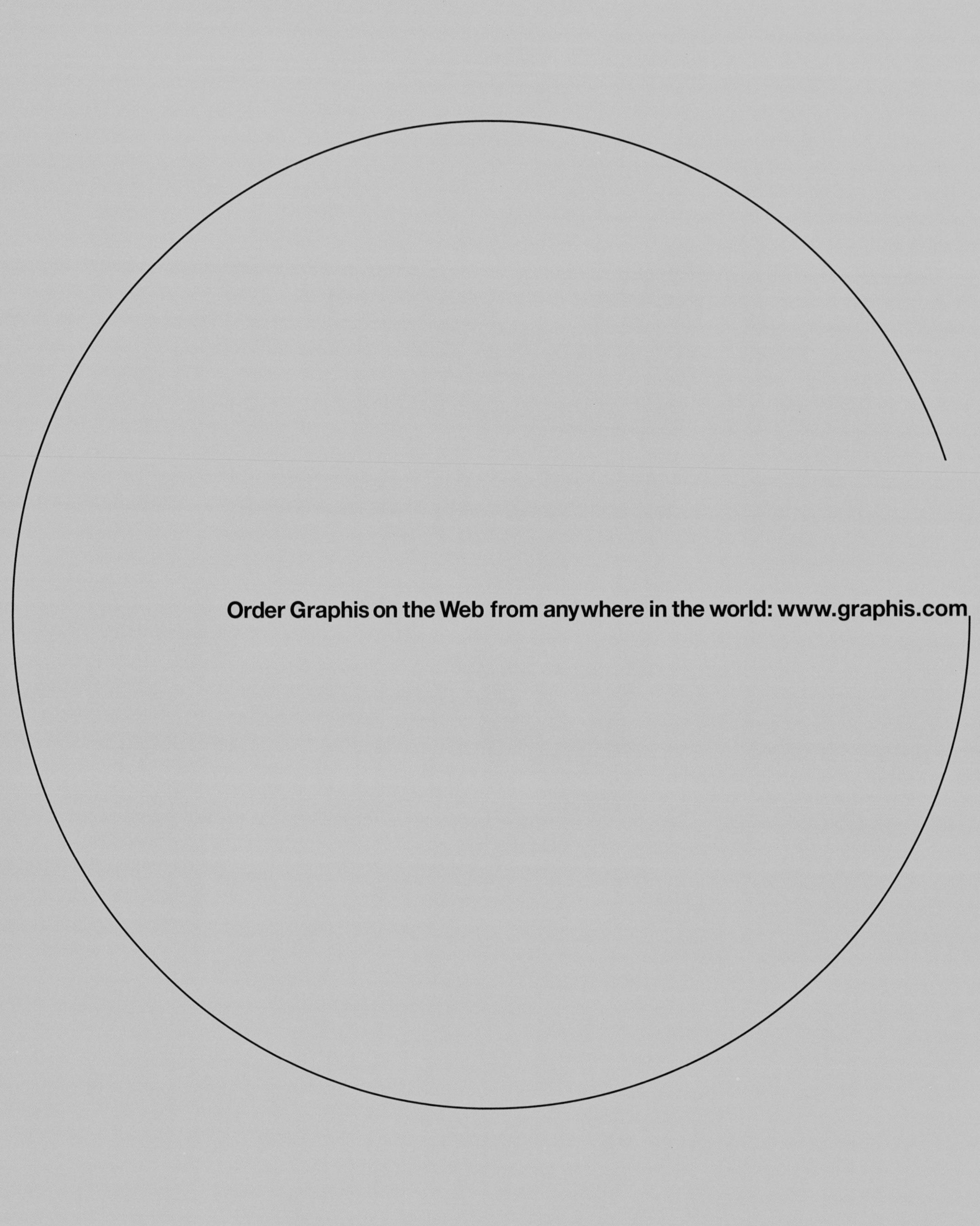
Order Graphis on the Web from anywhere in the world: www.graphis.com